RENOIR'S TABLE

SIMON & SCHUSTER
Rockefeller Center
1230 Avenue of the Americas
New York, New York 10020

Original title: *Renoir, à la table d'un impressioniste*
© 1994 Editions du Chène – Hachette Livre

Photographed by Jean-Bernard Naudin
Written by François Truchi, Jean-Michel Charbonnier,
Pierre Troisgros & Jacqueline Saulnier

ISBN: 0–671–89845–0

Printed and bound in Italy by Canale, Turin

10 9 8 7 6 5 4 3 2

Library of Congress Cataloging in Publication Data
Available Upon Request

RENOIR'S TABLE

The Art of Living and Dining with One of the World's Greatest Impressionist Painters

by

Jean-Bernard Naudin
Jean-Michel Charbonnier
Jacqueline Saulnier

Preface Pierre Troisgros

SIMON & SCHUSTER

New York London Toronto Sydney Tokyo Singapore

Acknowledgements

*We would like to extend our special thanks to Jacques Renoir
and Alain Renoir who enlightened us with their family memories.*

The editorial staff

*My particular thanks goes
to Louis Benzoni who helped on
every stage of this project,
as well as to Laurent Vigneron
and Barbara Guarneri. Mr. and Mrs. Nicolaï
helped out enormously at Les Colettes,
and I thank them.
Thanks also to Mr. Froumessole
and to Mr. et Mrs. de Bryas,
as well as François Truchi.*

Lydia Fasoli

Table of Contents

Pêches. Paris, Musée d'Orsay.

Preface

Artists have often proved to have precise ideas about cooking. In this, Renoir was no exception.

Many cooks feel close to visual art, and are always pleased with comparisons to the art of cooking. I was attracted to painting early on in life thanks to my father, who, despite a modest income, considered the buying of works of art important. I still have these tastes, and over the years I've managed to build a collection of Jean Puy paintings, another Impressionist of the period who is quite well known, and a native of Roanne as well.

I imagine that you, as I, admire and are fascinated by these young healthy women with their glowing complexions, the country dinners, the beautiful days whiled away on the river banks. Like myself, I am sure, you would enjoy them even more if you realized to what extent Renoir enjoyed life.

Renoir didn't have a large appetite, and he preferred simple and straightforward dishes. His social encounters and his travels shaped his "gourmet" life.

After his first meals as a painter in Barbizon, he discovered the cooking of the dance halls and the open-air cafés at the Fournaise restaurant with his future wife Aline, where cabbage soup and eel matelote were served alongside deep-fried gudgeon. The famous painting *Le Déjeuner des canotiers* gives us the flavor of these meals served on the water's edge.

Later, at the salons held by the Charpentiers, ardent supporters of the artists at the time, he was to be initiated into a more bourgeois cuisine. But his true nature would show on Saturday nights at his home in Montmartre, when the Renoir family would gather around a beef stew with friends. It was a strictly informal event— there was no need to call ahead, as it was an open door for all.

During this same period Renoir frequently dropped in to the Café Riche, where he was invited to eat by a collector friend who organized "Impressionist dinners". High-class cuisine such as mussel soup and shrimp sole would be served here, with "diplomat" fish being among his favorite dishes.

It would be wrong to forget Aline, who had set a goal of creating a cozy nest and healthy meals for Renoir, in order to give him the most serene atmosphere possible for his painting.

It was in his last home, Les Collettes in Cagnes, that he delighted in the cooking of Provence, particularly enjoying bouillabaisse, which had become his wife's speciality.

Through Jean-Michel Charbonnier's enchanting text the Impressionists' gentle style of living comes to life, and the chance to taste it for yourself. Thanks to the beautiful photographs by Jean-Bernard Naudin, the book is also a visual treat for art lovers. In short, it's a feast for the palate and for the eyes.

Thank you, Monsieur Renoir!

PIERRE TROISGROS

A Village Inn

*"Dinner was the day's big occasion; announced by the
setting sun, the dead juniper tree which served as the
inn's sign silhouetted behind its last red rays."*

Edmond et Jules de Goncourt

The year is 1915, and France is at war.
Pierre August Renoir and his son Jean,
who has come back from the front, are dining in
the artist's apartment on the Boulevard de
Rochechouart in Paris. The evening meal is
being served by Old Louise, the household cook.
Renoir, now confined to a wheelchair, worked a
full day in his studio before he was pushed into
the dining room this evening. Despite his poor
health, he hasn't lost any of his remarkable
energy for painting. Many people visit Renoir at
his home and they are constantly struck by the
sparkle in his eyes which are described by Jean as
"always laughing, always spotting the funny side
of things first." His appetite isn't what it used to
be, but Renoir wouldn't relinquish the ritual of
food and conversation for anything in the world.
These days, conversation at the dinner table often
takes on the tone of friendly bickering. Jean's
return has brought back Renoir's sense of humor,
and the painter seems to have shaken off the deep
depression he fell into following the death of his
wife, Aline. For the first time in a long while,
Renoir speaks candidly and sincerely. By nature

Located in Marlotte on the
edge of the Fontainebleau
forest, Le Cabaret de la mère
Anthony welcomed the
bohemian artists of the day.
Renoir stayed there
frequently in the 1860s,
along with Monet, Sisley,
and Bazille.

Le Cabaret de la mère Anthony
(detail). Stockholm National
Museum.

11

to settle in the French capital with his wife and four children; Renoir was four years old at the time. The journey by coach took more than two weeks, delayed at first by a brief dizzy spell that Renoir's little sister Lisa fell victim to. (She was later revived, thanks to an attentive postillion and a glass of brandy.) Upon arrival in Paris, the family settled into one of the Renaissance buildings in the Louvre courtyard which had been earmarked for destruction by the architect Visconti. The building was in the heart of old Paris, with its twisting narrow streets, mossy gables, and tiny gardens where lettuce was grown and picked fresh for the evening meal's salad. The Baron Haussmann was soon to replace this maze of crumbling city streets with the more orderly boulevards that now cut through Paris, but, in the meantime, Renoir played with his friends under Queen Amelie's windows. From time to time she would make a brief appearance to silence the boisterous children, kindly offering sweets that her lady-in-waiting passed around. Renoir also enjoyed the royal delicacies offered to him by one of Louis-Philippe's cooks, who was later to die tragically, gunned down during the 1848 revolution.

A great treat for Renoir during his childhood in Paris was to accompany one of the neighbors on hunting expeditions, running through wheat fields rich with fowl, that were later replaced by the Saint-Lazare train station and the surrounding European quarter. Renoir, however, was less fond of the annual spring pea harvest that had him trapped at home in the kitchen, shelling endlessly.

Renoir abandoned the family household to be apprenticed to a porcelain painter. There he began decorating vases and plates with portraits of Marie-Antoinette or of Venus amidst the

very discreet, even guarded, he now lets himself be carried away by his memories as they come flooding back. Whether it's about the wonderful meals he's enjoyed, or about his painting techniques, he speaks with the same enthusiasm, recounting some of the most delectable moments of his youth. Only the intermittent weeping of Old Louise interrupts his monologue. But it's a familiar sound to the family, and her tears have been held to blame whenever the soup is too salty.

Little is known about the early days of Renoir's life, which was spent in the Limousin region. Renoir's only memory is of moving in 1845, when his father, a stone craftsman, decided

clouds, work done so skillfully that he earned himself the nickname "Monsieur Rubens." After the studio closed, he painted the walls of a café on the Rue Dauphine with pagan gods, and followed that up with illustrations of more edifying scenes on screens used by missionaries. The destiny of "Monsieur Rubens" led him back to the Louvre, this time as a student copyist at the Ecole des Beaux-Arts, and to the studio of Gleyre, working side by side with Monet, Sisley and Bazille. Life was a whirl of café conversations, escapades in the studios and costume parties. This lasted until the spring of 1863, when Renoir and his comrades, on the advice of their professor, departed for the forest of Fontainebleau to sketch.

"Marlotte was made up of a few peasants' houses scattered around the junction of roads to Fontainebleau and from Montigny to Bourron. The woods stopped at the first houses on the northern side. Those on the south followed the Loing valley, where the wonderful river flowed just fast enough to shimmer, with majestic trees shading its banks. Corot immortalized the Loing river banks and Renoir and his friends often painted there. At Marlotte, their sense of poetic reality and their determination only ever to work with nature was reinforced, if that was possible. But none of them would yet take the step which would lead them to Impressionism. Between themselves and nature, many memories and traditions intervened. It was only after the war that they would "capture light and throw it directly on the canvas, to quote Monet," said Jean Renoir.

Above: Barbizon.
The Charmettes Hotel

13

The return to nature advocated by the Barbizon painters and their taste for the effects of light greatly influenced the Impressionists. But in contrast to Millet, Rousseau and Diaz de la Pena, who were happy to take sketches produced outdoors and work on them in their studios, Renoir and his companions worked directly on site. Careful to suppress any "romanticism" in their landscapes, they were not as fond of gnarled trees, deep ponds and dramatic cliffs as were their elders. A meadow filled with flowers or an apple tree in a suburban garden were enough for them.

Right: Frédéric Bazille, *Portrait de Renoir*, Paris, Musée d'Orsay.

Renoir spoke about this region so often and with such enthusiasm that his son Jean, the filmmaker, bought a house there and shot his first feature-length film, *La Fille de l'eau*, in the area. During his walks, Jean half expected to see Renoir "suddenly appear on a street corner, dressed in his painting smock, carrying his box of colors, his stool and his canvas, moving forward with long strides, his hand toying with his light brown goatee in the nervous gesture I know so well, his face still aglow from the presence of the fairies who kept him company in the woods." These fairies must have been slightly annoyed by the growing number of visitors to the forest. Indeed, in the middle of the nineteenth century, the woods were invaded by hordes of landscape artists. There were now more painters and tourists from the city than farmers who worked the land, if the satirical writers of the time are to be believed. La Fees pond, the Malmontagne chasm, La Roche Qui Pleure, the Brigands cavern and other picturesque sights soon became haunts for painters of the Barbizon school and a host of international daubers who were following in the footsteps of Millet and Théodore Rousseau. Renoir was less enthusiastic about knotted trees, deep ponds and dramatic cliffs than were his elders. Spending time at Chailly-en-Brière and Marlotte rather than at Barbizon, where "you would bump into Millets at every street corner," was a way of distancing oneself from the "sons of the enlightenment." It was also a way of spending less money. At the Cheval Blanc Inn in Chailly-en-Brière, a former post house run by Old Paillard, Renoir and his comrades from the Gleyre studio would spend less than four francs a day for adequate rooms and delicious meals. The group later took up room and board at the Lion d'Or hotel, located just across the street. The bacon omelet made by the hotel owner helped Renoir forget the one he ate so "heroically" in the company of Monet at the so-called Restaurant des Artists, an atrocious Barbizon eating establishment. Even more delectable moments took place in Marlotte, at the "tavern which is the Café Anglais of Marlotte, poetically named Anthony," wrote Ludovic Halévy, a friend of Degas, to his mother. But most of all, the tavern served as the setting for Renoir's first painting of a meal. At the time, this tiny village of small gray houses and charming rooftops was home to many quarrymen, woodcutters and farmers, and, in good times, the village would fill out with an invasion of rowdy painters, writers and musicians from Paris. A sprig of juniper served as the sign to the inn, the only one in the village. It was a small timber-framed house covered with ivy and clusters of roses and jasmine, looking on to a courtyard filled with a jumble of carts, and a motley assortment of cacophonous chickens and ducks. In 1866, the year Monet completed his *Déjeuner sur l'herbe*, a true manifesto of *plein air* painting, Renoir was placing his characters in the dining room of the inn. "I have wonderful memories of the painting *Le Cabaret de la mère Anthony*," he would tell the dealer Ambroise Vollard. "It's not that I find it particularly exciting, but it reminds me so much of the wonderful Old Madame Anthony and her inn in Marlotte which was the only real inn the village had." Old Madame Anthony makes a discreet appearance in the painting. She can be seen with her back turned, wearing a black kerchief. Her daughter Nana, famous for the "favors" she

would offer certain guests, is clearing white earthenware plates and coffee cups from the table. Pears and bread crusts still litter the table. Sisley, wearing a painter's smock and a hat, is leading the discussion. Jules Le Cœur listens attentively, rolling a cigarette. A copy of *L'Evénement* is in clear view on the table. In 1866, Zola wrote a series of articles in the paper defending Manet and criticizing the methods of selecting works for the annual Paris art show. His attacks were so ferocious there was a flood of letters of complaint from readers, and Zola was forced to quit before he had finished his series of articles. On the wall the portrait of Murger sketched in grisaille can be

made out. The author of *Scènes de la vie de bohème* sports a rifle on his shoulder, no doubt in reference to his feeble attempts at hunting that had made him a legendary figure in the village. It must be said, however, that the artists had huge appetites, whetted by long days spent walking in the forest. "The countryside is sport," Renoir used to say. He would sometimes walk the 37 miles from Paris to Marlotte, sleeping overnight in Essonnes. Most days, he would leave the inn at dawn wearing a wide-brimmed hat and his painting smock, carrying a folding chair and an umbrella for the sun. A packed lunch prepared by Madame Anthony—a crust of bread, a chicken leg, a piece of Brie and a flask of wine—would be carried in a wicker basket. Renoir wouldn't return to the inn until sunset. When the last lodger had returned, Nana would serve dinner in the commonroom. The walls and the doors were covered with portraits and landscapes by the artists who had given them in exchange for room and board. Several tables and long benches filled the room, and a dresser holding white earthenware dishes stood along one wall. In the chimney, a steaming pot of soup simmered on the coals and roasting fowls turned on the spit. Instead of eating omelets, the guests shared the partridges or woodcocks that the hunters brought back. The atmosphere was quite similar to that of the Auberge de Ganne described by Edmond de Goncourt: "People tossed their hats into the air, the large yellow cotton serviettes were thrown about, dogs were tied up to the leg of the chairs with string, and spoons clanged against the sides of the deep bowls. The big loaf of bread sitting on the piano was passed around with each person cutting off a slice, wine frothed in the glasses, forks dug into the food, plates were passed around, knives banged on the table in a demand

for seconds . . . and laughter broke out continuously." These happy moments were all the more intense for Renoir as he was sharing them with Lise Trehot, the love of his youth and his favorite model, whom he met at the home of his friend Jules Le Coeur in Marlotte. She is the young woman wearing a striking hat decorated with a feather, the bohemian with the dishevelled hair tenderly holding on to Sisley's arm. The young woman with the parasol, Renoir's first success at the Salon in 1868, is Lise as well.

*I*t was in 1874, on the Boulevard des Capucines at the home of the photographer Nadar, that the first exhibition was held of the group dubbed the "Impressionists" in jest. Along with Renoir's were paintings by Monet, Degas, Pissarro, Sisley, Berthe Morisot, Cézanne and Guillaumin. The painting *Chemin montant dans les hautes herbes* (around 1875) is a perfect example of the Impressionist vision, with Renoir reducing the human figure to a small black and white silhouette hidden in the vegetation. Trees are dotted discretely across the stretch of grass, brought alive by the red spots of poppies and an umbrella. In this world of sun and pleasure, linked to the memory of long walks in the Ile de France countryside, everything is a synthesis of color.

Left: *Le Cabaret de la mère Anthony.* Stockholm, National Museum. Above: *Chemin montant dans les hautes herbes.*

On the Banks of the Seine

*"By day, we savored this nearly animal desire for life that
arises from a wide, misty river, dazzled by light and
glorious weather . . . And then came the time for dinner,
the plentiful boat dinners: barbel cooked in butter and
matelote, served in the fishermen's cabins and the
abandoned ballrooms, hungers that could devour eight-
pound loaves and thirsts left by five hours of swimming . . ."*

Edmond et Jules de Goncourt

*I*t was 1869, the last peaceful summer of the
Second Empire. The banks of the Seine from
Argenteuil to Chatou were crowded with
holidaying Parisians, lured by the idea of a day in
the country, indulging in their love of long
walks, picnics and parties. An array of cafés
dotted the river's banks, but without a doubt
first prize went to La Grenouillère, on the Ile de
Croissy. That August, during a steamboat trip
down the river, Napoleon III and the Empress
Eugénie graced the café with their presence. For
the owner Seurin, it was the supreme honor.
Every guidebook to the countryside surrounding
Paris recommended his establishment, whether
for lunch, swimming, boating, or drinking and
dancing, with an occasional allusion to "frogs,"
referring not to four-legged amphibians but
rather to the young women of easy virtue who
were "not really prostitutes, but of that class of
free and independent girls who embraced the
values typical of Parisians at the time—changing
lovers at the drop of a hat, pursuing one fantasy
after another upon a whim, jumping rashly from
a private mansion on the Champs Elysées to an

*L*ocated on the Ile de
Chatou, a few hundred yards
from La Grenouillère (which
has since disappeared), the
Fournaise restaurant has
preserved a large part of its
nineteenth-century wall
decorations. It's the last
survivor of the number of
open-air cafés along the Seine
at the time of the
Impressionists. Renoir and
Maupassant regularly
frequented this fashionable
boating area which remained
in style long after the First
World War.

latter, as he took advantage of the small country house that his parents had recently purchased in Voisins-Louveciennes on the road to Versailles. The decor was sparse, to match the style of Madame Renoir herself, who disliked embellishments, wore only plain clothing and turned her nose up at creams and face powders. There were no heavy curtains at the windows, so as to allow the breeze and summer light to enter more directly. No knick-knacks decorated the house, apart from a few pieces of china painted by her son. The house opened out on to a small courtyard paved with stones and bordered by a garden. A good part of the fruits and vegetables of the orchard and the farmyard were given away to charity. Renoir was close to his family. During one extended visit, he painted a portrait of his father, Leonard, "a serious and silent man," and took long walks with his mother in the forest of Louveciennes and Marly. He also met up with Pissarro, whose family rented a home not far away, and the two whiled away the hours painting country roads, houses on the hillside, farm courtyards and vegetable gardens.

But most often Renoir visited Monet, who lived in a house on the hills of Bougival. At the time, Monet was flat broke, unhappy and more rebellious than ever. One day, when he was due to receive a visit from the banker and debt collector Ephrussi, Renoir stepped in to bail out his friend, who didn't have a single franc in his pocket. The painter then worked wonders with a rabbit taken from the family's hutch. He concocted a series of dishes with outrageous names that gave the special guest—a gourmet himself—the impression that he'd eaten a copious and succulent meal.

The two men went down to the banks of the Seine nearly every day to observe the vacationing

attic in Batignolles," recounted Jean Renoir. Frogs or not, as soon as good weather arrived, the Saint-Lazare train station was crowded on Sundays with women in summer dresses and men carrying wooden fishing poles and baskets of provisions. After a twenty-minute trip, a battalion of Parisians would be deposited at the train station in Rueil or Chatou, dizzy with wind and speed, hair dishevelled, and somewhat frazzled. Whether by foot or carriage, the travelers soon arrived at the water's edge and boarded the ferryboat that shuttled them to the island. For many, the pleasures of the river would only last a few hours; for the more fortunate, the whole of the warm season. Renoir was one of the

Parisians. They walked down the sloping streets of Bougival, strolled along the banks of the river bordered by villas, many of which were inhabited by artists, and crossed over the Bougival bridge. It took less than an hour to reach the Ile de Croissy and the highly fashionable baths at La Grenouillère. Rather than plant their stools on the park side of the island under the shade of its enormous trees, the two artists sat directly in front of the "floating café"—two firmly anchored barges on which a green and white wood hut with a balcony had been built. Along the river bank were boat houses, bathing huts in the thicket, summer cottages for rent and rustic-style tables and chairs under the shade of poplar trees.

Two footbridges led to the café, one of which crossed over a tiny rounded island where a single tree stood, nicknamed the "flower pot" or the "camembert." It was a required stop, giving men the chance to admire the ladies splashing about in the water, and women the opportunity to take in the men dressed in their striped swimsuits. The most daring would splash the absinthe drinkers who, in turn, shrieked in surprise. With the din of the café crowd in the background, the sideshow took place up and down the river. Maupassant, a boating enthusiast and a regular customer at La Grenouillère, never ceased to be amazed by the spectacle: "Fleets of yawls, skiffs, dinghies, canoes, ketches of all shapes and sizes,

*I*t was on the terrace of the Fournaise restaurant that Renoir painted *Le Déjeuner des canotiers* (1880–1881), with his friends posing as subjects. The friendly atmosphere of this place was described two years earlier by a journalist from *La Vie Moderne*: "Meals were chaotic: glasses were filled and then emptied with dizzying speed, the din of voices intermingled with the clatter of forks and knives in their raucous dance on the plates. A loud and heated drunkedness rose from the tables covered with debris and tottering bottles from the meal."

Le Déjeuner des canotiers.
Washington,
The Philips Collection.

sailed over the still waters, crisscrossing, tangling, bumping into each other, stopping abruptly before being pushed off again with a shove, sliding gracefully like long red and yellow fish . . . and laughter flashed over the water from one boat to the other; shouts, comments, slanging matches. The oarsmen exposed their bronzed and burnished forearms to the sun; and, at the back of the boats, parasols blossomed in red, green, blue and yellow, like strange flowers, like floating silken lilies."

Those boaters who proudly carried the title of "Grenouillards" were the most numerous. They would dip their oars in the water with a certain nonchalance, rowing calmly—unless they spotted a secluded area in the shade of a willow tree. Here they would consume a selection of delicious patés and cold meats, collapsing in the grass, giddy with wine and the afternoon heat.

Monet focused his attention on the glimmering sparkles of light dancing on the

surface of the water, while Renoir concentrated on the boats moored along the banks of the river, his paintbrush lovingly caressing the characters into shape on his canvas. He captured the details of both the bearing and the clothing of the holiday-makers, his strokes re-creating the marks left by their hair ribbons, the umbrellas, the hats of the elegant crowd, images quite different from the "blonde, improbably buxom women with exaggerated behinds, faces plastered with make-up, eyes rimmed thickly with kohl, blood-red lips, laced up and corseted in extravagant dresses," wrote Maupassant, "leaving a trail of garish bad taste as they passed over the fresh lawns."

Blind to this jaundiced vision, Renoir the beautifier was voyaging towards a modern Cythera, ingenuous shores from which the characters set sail, carefree, bathed in colored light and equipped with picnic baskets and wine. These are the river banks from which

*L*overs walking arm in arm; young women on swings; sweet nothings whispered under an arbor . . . during the Impressionist years, Renoir revived the atmosphere of the festive picnics of the eighteenth century. No one knew better than he how to capture the sensuality and relaxation of the open air, the joy of living on a brilliant summer's afternoon.

Sous la tonnelle, au Moulin de la Galette. Moscow, Pushkin Museum.

"Impressionism" developed, the term coined by an art critic in 1874 during an exhibition on the Boulevard des Capucines.

Renoir later abandoned the baths of La Grenouillère for another boating mecca, the Fournaise de Chatou restaurant, which he described in a letter to his friend Doctor de Bellio as "the prettiest place on the outskirts of Paris." Located at the base of a transport road linking Rueil to Chatou, the restaurant sat on the tip of the Grande Ile, a stronghold of the Fournaise family since the turn of the century. The head of the establishment was Alphonse Fournaise, or "the Grand Admiral," as he was affectionately known. Renoir would paint his portrait in 1875, the admiral seated in front of a glass of absinthe, his pipe clenched firmly in his teeth. The boating craze had helped turn Fournaise, a former shipwright, into a prosperous man. He built a handsome three-story freestone building next to his shops and construction site, which provided a comfortable apartment for his family. In addition to selling and renting boats, he organized regattas and jousting matches and gave guided tours of the river on a boat decorated with Chinese lanterns and garlands. For Parisians and vacationers, a day in the country meant enjoying a full meal by the water and so Fournaise launched himself into the restaurant business. He was helped by his wife, Louise, who kept a close watch on the kitchen, looked after purchasing and supervised the personnel.

Particular attention was paid to the restaurant's decor. It was located in a brick and stone building, and there was an extent of groves and grass arbors running along the riverbank and a balcony encircling the first floor, with the largest section directly facing the Seine. A sign illustrating the four stages of life hung on the facade of the entrance. It was the management's way of persuading guests to seize the moment. One panel depicted a baby boy playing with a rattle; the next a young man pulling petals off a daisy; after that, a swaggering, rather portly gentleman, and finally, an old man leaning on a cane. Above, the immobile hands of a *trompe-l'oeil* clock showed that time is frozen. Garlands strung from the balcony railings gave the restaurant an air of perpetual festivity. Further up, in the center

of the wall, a swimmer could be seen floating on a background of greenery. On the right, there was a soldier in a grenadier's uniform, standing to attention, his eyes fixed on a beautiful young servant. Other panels of the dining room wall were hung with drawings of boatmen and sailors, many of them left by painters as a token of thanks to the Fournaise family for their hospitality. Ironic verse by Maupassant scribbled on the wall cautioned diners on the dangers of abusing alcohol or the caresses of young women. The piles of carrots, turnips, lemon slices, asparagus and grapes in the kitchen were a hymn to the restaurant's cuisine. Indeed, Madame Fournaise's cooking attracted a steady and faithful clientele. Personalities from the world of politics, finance and show business, writers and painters, and people of all walks of life, came to feast for 100 francs per head. There was the traditional cabbage soup on Thursday nights, or the fish stew, the deep-fried gudgeon, goose roasted on a spit, artichokes from Louveciennes market gardens that were a delicacy at Les Halles food market in Paris, and the pear dessert—the delight of the gourmets in the French capital. The Argenteuil wine flowed freely, fueling the good-natured banter that came from the terrace, the ideal vantage point for watching small boats drift along the Seine.

An anecdote recounted by Edmond Renoir, the artist's younger brother, in the newspaper *La Vie Moderne* gives a good idea of what the atmosphere was like in the restaurant: "Two or three years earlier, some of the lodgers at the hotel, the posh sort, well-dressed, dug a pair of stuffy duchesses out of I don't know which high society who stayed for a few days, positioning themselves in the middle of all the boaters. Oh, did these women put on airs! Eating with their gloves, wanting to be called by their titles, fluttering about as though they were in the stuffiest of salons. The younger females present got it into their heads that they wanted these women out, and they proceeded to achieve this in the following manner: everyone put on gloves to eat, and called each other by the noblest of names imaginable. Ever since that day, whenever a newcomer behaves outrageously, the same strategy is used. The desired effect was inevitable."

This turbulent atmosphere seduced Renoir, who was introduced to the place by Prince Bibesco. "I was always there," the artist said one day to Ambroise Vollard. "There were as many beautiful girls there to paint as I could want . . . I took many clients to Fournaise's restaurant, and to thank me the owner commissioned his portrait, as well as one of his daughter Alphonsine." The girl's beauty had in fact won her a number of admirers. The clients praised her ingenuity, her doe eyes, her swimming skills and her charming conversation. She became one of Renoir's favorite models, appearing in one painting with her elbows propped up on a terrace table, sometimes wearing a bell-shaped hat, a bunch of cherries tucked behind an ear, her eyes staring dreamily off into space; other times she sported pieces of jewelry and wore her hair in curls. He painted her sitting in the back of a boat, her brown hair capped by a straw hat, and in an armchair, holding a fan.

Another young girl at the Fournaise restaurant caught Renoir's attention, and gradually monopolized his thoughts. She was Aline Charigot, a seamstress in Montmartre in her early twenties, who would become the central person in his life. He met her in 1880 in a dairy on the Rue Saint-Georges, where he regularly took his

meals. It was one of those neighborhood dairies where one could eat cheaply in a small room separated from the rest of the shop by a low partition. A regular clientele came for the daily specials of braised veal, lamb stew or beef with rock salt. Dessert consisted of a slice of Brie that Renoir called "the king of cheeses." "You can only find it in Paris," he used to say. "Beyond that barrier, it's no longer any good." Every week the dairywoman, a solidly built woman from Burgundy, would bring her friends together around a dish of kidney beans and bacon. They were vine beans she had brought in especially from Dijon—"the kind that push up between the stones, not that grow in fields like wheat or alfalfa in America." Renoir was one of the guests, the storeowner having decided she wanted him as a husband for one of her two girls. But the

"In Bougival at Souvent's place you're sure to remember
We must go there and right away
We must go back again
We'll wine and dine
we'll dance and sing
with Madame Fontaine et al!
Madame Fontaine et al!"

Above: Friture de guinguette, see recipe, page 140

painter only had eyes for Aline, a voluptuous creature with blond hair and a feline body. She had a button nose, full lips, almond eyes and, above all, delicate skin "that didn't reflect the light." Her features corresponded perfectly to the painter's canons. Everything about her seduced him: her light step, her way of gracefully pushing back a lock of hair that had strayed from her chignon that was "pinned up casually with no pretension." The Chatou restaurant would serve

interwoven than at the arbor of the Fournaise restaurant. The harmonious mixture of blue and orange would never be equaled. No one would ever paint with such happiness this sense of "Time standing still, filled with tenderness, intelligence and energy, where doing nothing at all gave us a feeling of living life to the fullest," which Marcel Proust wrote about. This scene of a trio of silent characters daydreaming the afternoon away, their boat floating languorously along the river, the mood free and easy in the state of torpor that follows a full meal, gave birth to the vivacious *Déjeuner des canotiers*, the suburban sequel to the *Bal du Moulin de la Galette*. This time, the scene is the terrace of the Fournaise restaurant, shielded from the sun by a red and gray striped awning. The models in the painting were all friends of Renoir, posing "when they had the possibility of going to Chatou." The execution of this "damn painting," one of Renoir's most ambitious undertakings, would take up most of his time from 1880 to 1881. Aline can be seen in the foreground wearing a wide-brimmed straw hat decorated with red flowers, pulling a face at her little dog perched on the table in the middle of the remains of the meal. On the tabletop is a sumptuous still-life scene of pears and grapes in a fruit bowl, bottles of wine, a small liqueur flask, glass bowls with long stems in which was served *mazagran*, cold black coffee mixed with seltzer water. Above Aline is the imposing figure of Alphonse, Fournaise's son, whom Maupassant describes in *La Femme de Paul* as a "strong, vigorous, red-bearded young man, who took the pretty young ladies by the hand while keeping these frail little boats delicately balanced." Across the table, the painter Caillebotte, dressed in a thin white jersey, is sitting astride his chair, and appears to be

as a backdrop for their love affair. Renoir took her canoeing and taught her how to swim. As she danced a marvelous waltz, he had her pose on the restaurant terrace in the arms of his friend Paul Lhote for the painting *La Danse à la campagne*. In *Canotiers à Chatou*, Renoir depicts her in bright sunlight about to step into a skiff manned by a young oarsman from the city. On the other side of the river the restaurant La Mère Lefranc and its shaded courtyard can be seen. And could Aline also be the young woman in a blue flannel dress with her elbows propped up on the table in *Déjeuner au bord de la rivière?*

In any case, the pleasures of boating and eating well would never be more inextricably

staring intensely at Aline. Next to him, the journalist Maggiolo, a writer for the satirical paper *La Triboulet*, leans toward Ellen Andrée, a blonde with charming features who seemed to be the preferred guest of the painters at the time. Degas invited her to lunch every week; Manet portrayed her as the young woman wearing a fedora, seated, in the two versions of *Au café*, and also as the fallen heroine of *L'Absinthe;* and finally Renoir had already painted her in *La fin du déjeuner* at a table in a Montmartre restaurant, a glass of liqueur in her hand as she watches her companion light up a cigarette. Charles Ephrussi, the wealthy collector, is also on the terrace of the Fournaise restaurant wearing a top hat. He is talking to a newcomer seated at the back of the terrace—Angèle, a Montmartre model used by Renoir, who is sipping from her glass. Pierre Lestringuez and Paul Lhote, both close friends of the painter, are in conversation with the actress Jeanne Samary of the Théâtre-Français, who is adjusting her hat with a black-gloved hand. Finally, there's Alphonsine Fournaise, leaning against the handrail as he listens to the Baron Barbier, a regular at the Folies-Bergères and the Moulin de la Galette dance hall. This relaxed and happy crowd brings to mind scenes from Renaissance banquets, like Veronese's love feasts. And whether they're wearing caps, boaters, straw hats, top hats, bowlers, or no hat at all, everyone seems to be on the verge of breaking into a song for Madame Fontaine.

*O*ften, after dinners at the Fournaise restaurant, the tables were cleared away and Alphonse sat at the piano. Aline, future wife of Renoir, danced with abandon in the arms of Paul Lhote, one of the painter's best friends.

Above: *Danse à la compagne*. Paris, Musée d'Orsay. Previous page: Bourdelots et douillons, see recipe, page 182

The Charpentiers' Salon

Madame,
I was to have lunch with you, which would have been an infinite
delight for me, as it has been so long since the last time. But I have
suddenly become a traveler, and have been gripped by a fever to see
the Raphaels. So I am devouring Italy. I started with the north, and
I will go all the way down the boot while I'm there, and when I have
finished I will celebrate properly by lunching with you.

A letter from Renoir to Madame Charpentier, 1882

During the 1879 Paris art show, one of Renoir's paintings created a sensation and marked the beginning of his success in high society. The *Portrait de Madame Charpentier et ses enfants* was described by Huysmans as "a work of a talented artist, who, despite his presence at the official Salon, is an independent." The model, whose right arm rests casually on the back of a flowered couch, displays a state of relaxation radically different from the others, and easily overshadows the fashionable women by Carolus-Duran and other portrait artists then in style in the Faubourg Saint-Germain district. The model in Renoir's painting was one of the most high-profile women in town, not only because she was the wife of Georges Charpentier, who published Flaubert, Zola and the Goncourt brothers, but also because she entertained the *crème de la crème* of the Paris literary, artistic and political worlds in her home. She held an eighteenth-century-style salon, hitherto obsolete, where all circles mixed. Talent rather than social class or money was the best calling card. Renoir had an abundance of it, and that was enough to make

Meeting the Charpentiers marked a decisive stage in Renoir's career. A regular at their home on the Rue de Grenelle, the painter came into contact with a clientele who commissioned numerous portraits from him, especially of wives and children, which assured him a certain financial security.

Jeune fille au chapeau blanc. London, Christie's.

him a regular visitor. He was unaffected, natural, and free from social ambition, although none of that was of any importance to the lady of the house. The reception she accorded him was extraordinary, even though he was little more than a obscure dauber in Montmartre when he began to frequent the salon. It was "a way of appeasing her husband's nostalgia for the bohemian life," according to Michel Robida in his book *Le Salon Charpentier et les impressionnistes.* Before marrying Marguerite Lemonnier, the daughter of an important jeweller of the Second Empire, and taking the reins of the famous publishing house founded by his father, Georges Charpentier—nicknamed Zizi by his friends because of a slight speech impediment—had often nursed his melancholy in the cafés of Batignolles and the baths of La Grenouillère. He dreamed of becoming a famous painter, but instead became the Impressionists' passionate supporter. He even launched the magazine *La Vie Moderne,* which Edmond Renoir, the artist's younger brother, would one day edit. Charpentier bought Renoir's first work in 1875, at an auction the painter organized at the hotel Drouot in collaboration with Monet, Sisley and Berthe Morisot. It was an auction that triggered an open attack from the critics. "The feeling the Impressionists give is that of a cat strolling along a piano keyboard, or of a monkey who gets his paws on a paint box," wrote the very influential Wolff in the newspaper *Le Figaro,* while at the same time showing a certain intuition at the end of his article: "Nonetheless, there is no doubt a good deal to be had for those investing in art of the future." The auction itself was turbulent. Students of the Ecole des Beaux-Arts created complete chaos and police officers had to be called in to restore order. The financial returns

were disastrous, but Renoir gained Charpentier's support. The editor bought *Le Pêcheur à la ligne* for the sum of 180 francs, and began inviting the artist to his Friday night parties. The Charpentiers had recently moved to the Rue de Grenelle, in the Faubourg Saint-Germain quarter, and were living in an apartment located above the offices of the publishing house. Renoir became "the most devoted of ordinary painters" to the Charpentiers, as he liked to call himself in his letters, in a reference to the *Grand Siècle.* Madame Charpentier commissioned a portrait from him, which she hung over the mantelpiece in the living room, as well as a decoration for the stairwell (two narrow panels which faced each other depicting a man and a woman leaning on a ramp), and ornaments for her large mirror frames. Madame Charpentier's dinners provided an opportunity for the painter to meet not only art lovers, who would soon submerge him with commissions, but also writers, actors and politicians—a world which until then had been alien to him. There was nothing Renoir loved better than to be surrounded by gourmets and indulge in "food talk," Zola being in this respect a perfect guest. Trembling with joy at the thought of the clams that were to be served, the writer described in detail his shopping expedition to some of the city's best produce markets. Zola had such an extensive knowledge of the science of cooking that he was able to whisper into his neighbor's ear exactly how many minutes more a particular dish should have simmered for it to be

*T*he exquisite fare and scintillating conversation of the guests made Madame Charpentier's dinners the most coveted of the Parisian literary and artistic scene.

Right: Rissoles à la Chevreuse, see recipe, page 146.

*A*n honored guest of the Charpentier's, Renoir was even in charge of creating one of the dinner menus. One evening, the guests were served a Belle Suisse soup, salmon trout with shrimp sauce, lamp chops with morel mushrooms, *capon a la Montesquieu*, duck

Rouennaise, Parisienne ham, and, to help digest it all, Musotte ice cream.

Right: Bar poché aux écrevisses, see recipe page 150.

perfectly cooked. He waxed lyrical over dishes his wife prepared for him at his house in Médan, and spoke excitedly about his love of Lappland reindeer tongue. Turgenev, another regular at the salons, praised the taste of Russian snipe, which he considered the best game in the world, or reminisced about a marvelous bottle of Rhine Valley wine, opened ceremoniously in a German inn by a golden-tressed Gretchen. The jovial atmosphere of these weekly social gatherings is captured in an anecdote recounted by Jean Renoir. One day, when his father was sketching in the Marly forest, he suddenly remembered that he was invited to a formal dinner that evening at the Charpentier household. Having missed the regular passenger train to Paris, he jumped on to a baggage car which came to a stop in the marshalling yard of the Batignolles station, hailed a carriage home, and hastily dressed for the evening. He arrived at last at the Charpentiers' apartment, handing his top hat, his scarf and his gloves to the butler with great formality. He took off his overcoat, walked into the living room and was greeted by bursts of laughter: he had forgotten to put on his dinner jacket and was dressed only in shirt-sleeves. Far from feeling offended, Charpentier took off his jacket as well. One by one, the other guests did the same, including the statesman Léon Gambetta, the guest of honor at these gatherings. Madame Charpentier had to pull strings among the most influential people in Paris to secure him as a guest at her table, and his last-minute acceptance only heightened her terror that the meal might be overcooked. Georges Charpentier wanted Gambetta to meet Renoir to secure a commission

for the artist for a panel for the Hôtel de Ville in Paris, but the deal was unsuccessful. Surprised at the refusal, Renoir declared, "It's the only style of painting that matters today; the artists whose works are being commissioned are worthless." "But it's better to see the Republic live with bad painting than to see it die with great art," Gambetta retorted, after gently accusing Renoir of being a "revolutionary."

Feigning an exaggerated awkwardness to hide his inexperience in the ways of high society living, Renoir remained slightly aloof during these evenings, just as he did during conversations at the Café Guerbois or the Nouvelle Athènes. The artist was entertained and fascinated by the gallery of characters he rubbed shoulders with in the salons, and he would study the guests with interest: the mistress of the

household, with her regal bearing and her favorite choice of dress at the costume balls which had earned her the nickname "Marie-Antoinette." ("Marie-Antoinette in miniature," whispered some people, referring to her small size.) She reminded Renoir of his teenage romances and the models painted by Fragonard. Then there was the Duchesse d'Uzès, whose mansion was next door to the Charpentiers' residence; Flaubert, whom he said "had the appearance of a retired captain turned travelling wine salesman"; Barbey d'Aurevilly, his evening dress emblazoned with a red sash; Edmond de Goncourt, lost in thought, taciturn, referred to behind his back as "the widow" ever since the death of his brother Jules. Renoir was as intrigued by the extravagant dress of the fashionable painter Carolus-Duran, nicknamed Caracolus-Carocolant, as he was by

Regarding a portrait of Madame Charpentier and her children which created a stir at the salon of 1879, Marcel Proust wondered in *Le Temps retrouvé:* "Isn't the poetry of an elegant home and the beautiful clothing of our times better recorded for posterity in the salon of the publisher Charpentier painted by Renoir rather than in the portrait of Sagan or the countess of La Rochefoucauld by Cotte or Chaplin?"

Portrait de Madame Charpentier et ses enfants. New York, The Metropolitan Museum of Art. Wolfe Fund, 1907. Catharine Lorillard Wolfe Collection.

the thick Alsatian accent of the painter Henner and the Provençal accent of Alphonse Daudet, one of the most gluttonous of the lot.

The Charpentiers' luxurious apartment provided the artist with emotionally charged images: candlelight flickering playfully across the rich fabrics, the impressive array of objects, the muted atmosphere created by the heavy drapes, the deep shadows in the rooms. The reception rooms were decorated with Japanese curiosities, which Charpentier collected devotedly. The apartment overflowed with embroidered satins, silks stitched with multicolored flowers, screens, and china purchased at Desoye, a shop on the Rue de Rivoli where artists stocked up on etchings, screens and kimonos for their models. The craze for Japanese curiosities reached its height in

*T*he theme of young girls at the piano was one of Renoir's favorite subjects. As in a number of such paintings, the dark-haired girl here is dressed in pink and the blonde is wearing a white frock with a blue belt. There is an atmosphere of youthful harmony in a pastoral setting. In 1892, the year the government purchased one of the versions of *Jeunes Filles au*

piano, the painter Maurice Denis wrote: "He knows how to interpret his own emotions, find nature and the dream state in his own way: he draws wonderful bouquets of women and flowers with his own joy of vision."

Jeunes filles au piano. Paris, Musée d'Orsay.

1878, the year of the World Exhibition that was held on the Champ de Mars. The Japanese House near the Trocadéro was all the rage, particularly its screen with the silver heron motif. To mark the event, the Charpentiers gave a dinner with a Japanese theme, with dishes brought over from the Japanese restaurant at the exhibition. "The Japanese had made everything themselves: small fish tarts, white and green jellied fish, and a dish they seemed quite fond of—small rice rolls wrapped in grilled seaweed, like a piece of white sausage wrapped in a black sausage," remembered Edmond de Goncourt, who was part of the dinner party. After the meal, the two Japanese cooks, who were also artists, did rough ink sketches on pieces of material, including three crows which particularly delighted the crowd. Although he was influenced less by the Japanese fashion than were the other Impressionists, Renoir admired the relationship the Japanese had with nature.

"They still have that simplicity of being that allows them the time to go out and contemplate life," he wrote in a note found later by his son. "They still look with wonder at a blade of grass, the flight of a bird, or the marvelous movements of a fish, and go home full of lovely ideas that they apply with ease to the object they're painting." Renoir willingly fell in with fashion by painting Madame Charpentier in the middle of the exotic decor of her smoking room. In the background, there were kimonos adorned with peacocks, alternating with bands of cherry-red silk. The craftsmanship was so sumptuous that it was difficult to say which was the more riveting: the long evening gown by Worth with its lace train that perfectly matched the fur of Porto, her Saint-Bernard, or the glowing complexions of the children, Georgette and Paul.

The Pot-au-Feu

"I was born at the Château des Brouillards on 15 September, 1894, slightly after midnight. The midwife presented me to my mother, who said, 'My good Lord, he's ugly! Take him away!' My father said 'What a mouth! It's a veritable oven! He's going to be a pig . . ." Unfortunately, he was right."

Jean Renoir

In 1890, several months after marrying Aline, Renoir moved to the Rue de Girardon in a section of Montmartre with the lovely name of Château des Brouillards. Living there was like being in the countryside. From the folly erected in the eighteenth century by the farmer-general Lefranc de Pompignan, all that remained was an edifice with a crumbling facade topped with a pediment and surrounded by the tall trees of the park. Now, two-story wooden houses lined the roadway that had replaced the common grounds of the château. Renoir's family settled into one of the buildings. It was an enchanting environment for Renoir, with its small garden filled with plum and lilac trees, the country hedge hidden by tangled rose bushes and the lingering memories of formal garden parties held in Watteau's day. The attic of the house was transformed into a studio; from here, Renoir could see the hilltops of Meudon, Argenteuil and Saint-Cloud. On clear days, he could even make out the Saint-Denis basilica. He painted the common rooms of the house in white and the doors in Trianon grey, "which required a

*I*n this photograph taken in 1895 by Martial Caillebotte, the brother of the painter Gustave Caillebotte, Renoir is sitting on the steps of his house at the Château des Brouillards in Montmartre. His home was open to all for dinner every Saturday, when his friends would show up to share a pot-au-feu.

top-quality linseed oil, with the white mixed with bone-black, not peach black." Some of the glass panes of the dining room were decorated with scenes from classic mythology. As the house had been constructed with lightweight materials and was quite humid, Renoir set up a stove in the attic of the type that was the latest in modern comfort.

In 1894, his second son, Jean, was born. "What a mouth he has! It's a veritable oven! He'll be a pig!" the painter exclaimed when he laid eyes on his latest offspring. To celebrate the birth, Aline called upon Madame Mathieu, who was both laundress and cook, to prepare baked tomatoes "according to one of Cézanne's recipes," adding in a good dose of olive oil. It was a great success, judging by the reaction of Abel Faivre, one of Renoir's closest friends, who, in tasting the recipe for the first time, cleaned his plate so thoroughly that he nearly wiped the pattern off the dish. Madame Mathieu was called upon to provide another round.

It was at this time that Gabrielle Renard, a cousin of Madame Renoir, arrived from Essoyes to look after the children. She was fifteen years old and had received a thorough education at the convent. But she could also "guess the year of a wine, catch trout with her bare hands without being caught by the local policeman, look after the cows, help bleed the piglet, pick grass for the rabbits and clear away droppings left by the horses when they returned from the fields," said Jean. Gabrielle would become one of the painter's favorite models, and she stayed with the family until 1914, two years before the death of her "boss." She left to marry the American painter Conrad Slade, and spent the rest of her life in California. In Renoir's family portrait painted in 1896, set in the garden of the Château des Brouillards, she can be seen crouched down next to Jean and wearing a lace dress. Aline is wearing one of the extravagant hats Renoir was so keen on, which he often had custom-made for his models. The eldest son, Pierre, a budding Don Juan, has his eyes on a young neighbor.

Indeed, the entourage of the Renoir family was utterly charming. Madame Brebant, the landlady, dressed as though it were still the Second Empire, and was always followed close at heel by two Italian greyhounds who yapped incessantly. The two canines so annoyed Renoir that he commented quite clearly that he approved of "the Chinese practice of eating dog." The concierge, Madame de Paillepre, was married to a ruined Marquis. She would take the garbage out, then, moments later, would stroll along the road wearing a full-length dress as was the style at the time, pretending to fan herself. Then there was Blanchette, the newspaper man's simple-minded sister who, at forty years of age, played blind man's bluff with the children in the neighborhood. The laundress, who was well known to be quite fond of absinthe, would let laundry fall into the gutter. Renoir painted in the garden; Aline did her sewing; a neighbor stopped by to describe the latest melodrama at the Montmartre theater; and Madame Alexis, the wife of the poet and journalist, read aloud descriptions of her travels, unless Bibi La Purée, the poet of the underworld, stopped by to recite a few verses in exchange for a slab of cold meat and a couple of gherkins—emptying the jar in the end, as well as the bottle of wine that went with it.

Jean Renoir remembers the jovial atmosphere that reigned at the Château des Brouillards: "We never paid visits to one another but we saw each other all the time. There was never any formal

invitation to lunch or dinner. But people would say, 'I've got an extra veal steak, how does that sound?' And if the other person nodded in agreement, another place was set at the table. Women at the Château des Brouillards never stood around chatting idly. They were always busy, bursting into a neighbor's kitchen unannounced to ask for a sprig of chervil, or to bring over a sample of the wine their husbands had freshly bottled."

Renoir went past the underworld of the "maquis" several times a day to get to his second studio on the Rue Tourlaque at the foot of the hill. Located on the north side of Montmartre between the Moulin de la Galette and the Rue Caulaincourt, the maquis was a wide area covered in hawthorn bushes where Gabrielle collected snails. Wooden shacks erected in a haphazard

way housed a colorful group of outsiders, artists and tramps. There were tiny gardens, where many of the inhabitants raised hens, rabbits and even goats. There was a woman among the crowd named Josephine, a fishmonger who left for Les Halles market each morning and then returned to sell her goods in the streets of Montmartre. Aline placed her orders for herring with Josephine; it was one of Renoir's favorite fishes. They were grilled on a charcoal fire, then served up with a delicious mustard sauce. Not too far from Renoir's house there was an orchard which belonged to one of the last farmers left in Montmartre. Here, Renoir's family would collect unripe, tart-tasting little pears. There was even a field nearby with several cows, and Gabrielle would go to get fresh milk from the small house that bordered it.

In general, stores were rare on the hill. A shopping excursion required a walk down to the Rue Lepic, "where costermongers lined up their small wagons of fruits and vegetables," and sometimes one had to venture even further to the Rue des Abbesses. For special occasions, Renoir ordered a vol-au-vent or a pâté at Bourbonneux, and he hand-picked his brioche from the pastry store. On Good Friday Aline prepared her famous bouillabaisse, using scorpion fish, small crayfish and sprigs of fennel, all ordered directly from Marseilles and picked up by one of the servants from the Gare de Lyon.

The Château de Brouillards was in fact quite out of the way. The omnibus stopped at the Boulevard de Rochechouart and hackney cabs would often refuse to venture up into the maze of small streets in upper Montmartre. But the distance didn't stop close friends from arriving in swarms to share Madame Renoir's traditional Saturday night pot-au-feu. There was no need to send out invitations, or to give people advance notice. Everyone knew that the Renoirs' home was open to anyone every Saturday, a tradition established by the painter's mother. "If no one showed up, we were obliged to eat boiled meat for the rest of the week," Renoir said, reflecting on his childhood. Now it was Aline's turn to rally the servants, models and children to prepare the gherkins which accompanied the meal. The pot-au-feu was cooked on a charcoal-burning kitchen stove, a style of cooking that was being used less and less frequently in Paris. The stove consisted of square grills set on a sort of earthenware plate with a ventilation shaft above. Ash would fall into a compartment closed with a small metal

Gabrielle Renard, Madame Renoir's cousin, arrived at the painter's home in 1894 to help with housework and look after the second son, "little Jean." Gabrielle was one of Renoir's favorite models and would stay with the family until 1914, when she married the painter Conrad Slade. She left France at the beginning of the Second World War to live in Los Angeles, not far from Jean Renoir.

Right: *Gabrielle et Jean.*
Paris, Musée d'Orsay.

Left: Le Château des Brouillards in Montmartre.

Next page: *Pommes et poires.*
Paris, Musée d'Orsay.

door that could be adjusted for changing the draw. The fire was kindled using small sticks, the tips having been soaked in resin. Charcoal was then added, which would be covered with a *diable*, a sort of inside-out funnel topped with a pipe that activated the draw.

When the pot-au-feu was ready, everyone would find a place at the table without ceremony. Among the regulars was the journalist Paul Alexis, a neighbor on the Rue des Brouillards. A fervent supporter of Impressionism, and bubbling over with energy and enthusiasm, Alexis wrote articles in slang for the newspaper *Le Cri du Peuple*, which Renoir enjoyed immensely. Ambroise Vollard frequently made the climb up to the "Château." He too had a strong appreciation for good food: he transformed the cellar of his gallery into a dining room and served up delicious and spicy Creole dishes, delighting the painters with curried chicken, coconut crab and cabbage. The closest friends at the Saturday meals were Lestringuez, Georges Rivière, the

musicians Chabier and Cabaner, and the painters Franc-Lamy and Cordey. The dinner guests reminisced about the dinners the pastry-chef used to give every first Wednesday of the month in the back room of his store on Boulevard Voltaire, which Renoir had decorated with painted wreaths of flowers and leaves. After the fall of the Commune, Parisians, deprived of sweet foods, were devouring desserts and sweets, and Murer's business was instantly successful. He raced from one gallery and auction room to another filling orders for vol-au-vents or—his speciality—cream puffs. He bought paintings from Pissarro, Renoir, Monet and Sisley, and invited them to dinners held in his store's back room where the walls were covered with shiny pots and pans, and baking tins of unusual shapes.

His guests have a wonderful memory of the raffle he organized, with the first prize—a painting by Pissarro—going to a maid who worked in the neighborhood. When she ran up to claim her prize with ticket in hand, a look of horror came over her face when she saw the painting. Pointing at an enormous Saint Honoré cake in the window, she exclaimed "If I had my choice, I'd rather have that!"

Dining with the Impressionists

"Members of the bourgeoisie, men of letters, bankers and dandies, actors and artists, everyone in Paris who knows how to live elegantly and comfortably, lovingly haunted, haunts and will haunt the Café Riche."

Alfred Delvau

*R*enoir spent many moments of his youth in heated discussions over inexpensive meals at restaurants devoid of mirrors and gilding, like the Nouvelles Athens on the corner of the Place Pigalle; the Brasserie des Martyrs, on the street of the same name; or the Café Guerbois, on the Avenue de Clichy. But success brought invitations from Georges Charpentier, Paul Berard, Charles Ephrussi and other wealthy collectors to dine at the famous Tortoni restaurant on the Boulevard des Italiens. Upstairs, in the spacious and brightly lit dining room, a sumptuous buffet offered an array of cold cuts, jellied meats, shellfish, and chilled chicken fricassée, the house speciality. Dandies lunched there, enjoying plates of truffled rice, papillotte of young hare, salmon steak, and beef tenderloin Neapolitan-style. Elegantly-dressed Parisians stepped down from their carriages to be seated at one of the outdoor tables next to the pyramids of ice cream and pretty baskets of waffles. "Tortoni was *the* boulevard, almost fame itself!" Renoir would comment later to Vollard. Indeed, according to one observer of Parisian life in the

*I*n the nineteenth century the wide boulevards were the center of Parisian life. Some of the capitals most famous restaurants and cafés were here: the Maison Doré, the Café Helder, the Café Anglais, Tortoni and the Café Riche. Here, too, near the opera were the theaters and luxury boutiques, and the galleries where Renoir and his Impressionist friends exhibited their paintings.

mid-nineteenth century, "the Boulevard des Italiens is the center of the world, the be-all and the end-all, the ultimate goal of everyone's efforts, the last word in ambition. It's here that one must burst forward into the limelight on the boulevard's sidewalks, secure a spot even though there's hardly room to breathe, become famous, acquire a name, a number, something!" Renoir of course was no Rastignac, but he detested the new residential neighborhoods in the west of Paris ("a very nice cemetery, but I prefer Père-Lachaise," he said of Neuilly) and relished far more the glittering life of the boulevards, with their wide-open spaces, lights, and crowds strolling along the wide sidewalks past luxurious shop windows and squeezing into the Vaudeville or the Opéra-Comique. The leaves on the trees along the boulevard disguised the banality of the

architecture and the tediousness of the Haussmann buildings that are "cold and lined up like soldiers." Renoir and the other Impressionists were so attached to the neighborhood of the *grands boulevards* that most of their shows took place there; for their dealers, the address was a highly prosperous one. Paul Durand-Ruel and Ambroise Vollard had their studios on the Rue Laffitte. Georges Petit was on the Rue de Seze, at the beginning of the Boulevard des Capucines. The headquarters for the revue *La Vie Moderne*, founded by Charpentier and edited by Renoir's brother Edmond, was located on the Boulevard des Italiens. After private openings in the evenings, painters and clients met up at one of the many café terraces, where Manet so often positioned his heroines, absinthe drinkers or women dreamily eating plums in *eau-de-vie*. The best tables in the city were found here. Lining the Boulevard des Capucines were the Café Americain, the Grand Café, the Grand Hotel Café. And along the Boulevard des Italiens were the no less famous restaurants the Maison Doré, the Café Helder, the Café Anglais and the Café Riche.

Located at the corner of the Boulevard des Italiens and the Rue le Peletier, the Riche had been a haven for gourmets since the Second Empire. Offenbach had his own table there, Ferdinand de Lesseps found himself sitting next to Gustave Doré, Alexandre Dumas *père*, or the tragic actress Rachel. Maupassant brought along his *bel ami*, and Zola dazed his little sweethearts with iced punch and champagne frappé. Only the war of 1870 interrupted the feasts. Radishes with butter and horse sausage replaced the mussel soup, fish with diplomat sauce—the house delicacy—sole with shrimp (the favorite dish of the women of easy virtue), accompanied by red Bouzy, crayfish with bordelaise sauce, woodcock *à la Riche*, lamb chops on a bed of asparagus tips or partridge flanked by quail.

The Riche was unsurpassed in its magnificent décor. A marble staircase with brass railings led upstairs to eight rooms, where guests dined by the light of candles set in tall candelabras, surrounded by Roux furniture in the Boulle style, Barbedienne bronzes and Persian plants. The walls were panelled in onyx or covered in red brocade, and Aubusson carpets were strewn on the floor. In his book *La Curée*, Zola described the white dining room as "a room tiled in white and gold, furnished with all the coquetries of the boudoir," with a large divan, virtually a bed, between the fireplace and the window. "A clock and two Louis XVI candlesticks graced the white marble mantelpiece. But the room's most curious

object was the mirror, a beautiful broad mirror on which these women with diamonds had scribbled names, dates, mangled verses, striking thoughts and astonishing confessions." The Riche kitchen was another curiosity, as huge as a cathedral, white and luminous, described in detail in Parisian guidebooks. A gigantic pantry and a *sommellerie* arranged like a desk separated it from the cellars which held its treasures. These included "red Côtes d'Or from 1811—when one of these half-century-old bottles was found to be still drinkable, it was ecstasy to taste—1819 Sauternes, admirably preserved, a prodigious 1842 Romanée, an 1848 Léoville-Barton, indisputably the best of the three. Then the best

and largest collection of 1858 *grands crus* Burgundies, a vintage whose splendor has been forgotten. Of foreign wines, there were authentic Steinbergs and Johannis-bergs [sic], Tokay-Esterhazy, Madeira wine of unknown age which was like bottled life; a Sicilian wine, 1820 Marsala San Donato, etc., and the rest of it up to this standard. Whichever way you looked at it, it was a house of the first order. Others could equal it; none could surpass it."

Doctor de Bellio organized his "Impressionist dinners" at this gourmet temple. He had been friends with Renoir and other painters in the group for nearly twenty years. A doctor of Romanian extraction, de Bellio was a dilettante and one of the first collectors of Impressionist work, backing the artists generously even during their most difficult moments. "Any time any one

of us needed money quickly, we ran to the Riche at lunchtime," Renoir would later tell Vollard. "One was certain to find Doctor de Bellio, who would buy one of our paintings without even looking at it." Later, when de Bellio's purchases became less frequent, he would help the painters by recommending them to his friends or family. In the early 1890s he tried to reunite former members of the group for monthly meetings at the Riche. It was a difficult task, as most were on bad terms and others were by then no longer resident in Paris. Degas was angry with everyone; Cézanne was living in Aix-en-Provence; and Sisley was in Moret-sur-Loing, in the Fontainebleau region.

On May 6, 1892, in a private dining room on the second floor of the Riche, de Bellio held a dinner to celebrate Renoir's exhibition at the

Durand-Ruel gallery, a complete retrospective which brought together more than one hundred works of art.

The painter was enjoying an immense success at the time. A month earlier, the state had bought his painting *Jeunes filles au piano*, to exhibit at the Luxembourg Museum. Durand-Ruel's clients were going wild over his paintings of young girls in fancy hats, innocent young things in summer dresses and flowered bonnets, seated in fields, picking wildflowers, strolling through the sun-drenched countryside or strumming on the piano in a cozy interior scene. His still-lifes of gladioli in vases or grapes and peaches on tabletops were earning him much praise from the critics. "He knew to limit himself to those emotions within his own domain, interpreting nature and dreams in his own way." "It is with a certain joy of vision that he composes these marvelous bouquets of women and flowers."

At this dinner, he most certainly discussed his upcoming trip to Spain with Paul Gallimard, the head of the Théâtre des Variétes and an important art collector. He would also have spoken of the paintings by Velásquez in the Prado museum he had wanted to see for so long. The eighteenth century was a subject of great debate, whether about Watteau or Fragonard. Monet, at the height of his success, was one of the guests at the table. American collectors were fighting over his paintings. He had bought his home at Giverny the year before, and he had just finished showing his *Peupliers* at Durand-Ruel's gallery. Also at the table was the critic Théodore Duret, an ardent supporter of the movement, and an enthusiast of Japanese art.

Renoir met Mallarmé at Berthe Morisot's home during one of the Thursday evening

"*L*et's not forget the sauce, this restaurant's famous sauce, which is neither the *sauce au fumet*, the *sauce au blanc*, the *sauce Robert*, the *sauce velouté*, the *sauce béchamel*, the *sauce perlée*, the *sauce au pauvre homme*, the *sauce à la bonne femme*, the *sauce salmis*, not any of these but quite simply the sauce of the Café Riche, and the secret of its head chef."
Alfred Delvau, *Les Plaisirs de Paris.*

Left: Pièce de boeuf lardée et rôtie, see recipe page 168.

TÉLÉPHONE 218-88   « AU PETIT RICHE » — Restaurant à la Carte
25, Rue-Le Peletier
POUR OFFRES DE SERVICE JUSQU'A 2 HEURES

*L*ocated in the quarter of the *grands boulevards*, near the famous Café Riche (which has since disappeared), Le Petit Riche at the time was a restaurant and a wine depot specializing in the wines of Bourgeuil and Vouvray. It has preserved its 1880 décor of beautiful mirrors engraved with bowls of fruit, and painted ceilings bordered by a frieze of fruit and vegetables.

Right: Diplomate Belle Epoque, see recipe page 183.

gatherings, *soirées* that were renowned as much for refined cooking and the wide variety of dishes, including an excellent rice *à la Mexicaine* and date chicken, as for the stimulating company of the guests.

A strong friendship had developed between the painter and the writer, captured perfectly in a photograph taken by Degas at the home of Berthe Morisot, showing Mallarmé leaning against the wall next to "Monsieur Renoir, who is far from feeling blue at the sight of a bare shoulder." Despite the presence of the writer, known as "the peacemaker," who seemed to have a calming effect on those engaged in debate around him, they couldn't make it through the meal without at least one amusing episode due to the perpetual tension between Renoir and Caillebotte. Renoir had come armed with an encyclopedic dictionary, firstly to be informed on the many subjects brought up at the table, and secondly to have one over on his friend. The artist was "highly strung and sarcastic, his voice mocking in tone, a sort of devilishness marking

his face which was ravaged by illness, with an ironic twist and a bizarre laugh." According to the novelist Gustave Geoffroy, another regular at the Impressionists' dinners, Renoir "took malicious pleasure in annoying him." After dinner, friendly arguments continued down on the boulevard amidst the hubbub of the crowds of evening strollers, with discussions concluding over a glass of beer at a café terrace.

Two years after that dinner with Renoir the Café Riche was transformed into a brasserie, and these wonderful extravagances would be no more. This was much to the chagrin of Edmond de Goncourt, who would write in his *Journal*: "Never have I seen anything as positively vile as the new décor of the Café Riche, with Forain's gruesome frescoes and Raffaelli's colored caryatids, in this muddle of oriental architecture in a Renaissance-Faubourg-St-Antoine style. Oh, where are my wonderful old cafés, my old restaurants, in simple gold and white . . ."

Family Life

"I am becoming more and more a man of the country, and I'm beginning to notice, although rather late in life, that winter is the real season, with the fires alight in the enormous fireplaces soothing the mind. The blaze is merry, and the wooden clogs on your feet keep the cold at bay. And then there are the chestnuts and the potatoes roasting under the coals, accompanied by a little bottle of Côte d'Or."

Letter from Renoir to Manet, December 29, 1888

Aline wanted her husband to be surrounded by a calm and comforting atmosphere to help him to create in the best conditions possible. The idea was to build a cozy nest in Essoyes, her native village bordering the Champagne and Burgundy regions.

Renoir had two obstacles to overcome, the first being the opinion of Aline's mother. Madame Charigot had difficulty with her daughter's union with a "good-hearted starving artist." Second, Renoir hesitated at making the leap to such a different way of living. "You have to be extremely strong to isolate yourself!" he said. The 1880s were a period of questioning for the artist. Feeling at a standstill and doubting Impressionism more and more, he embarked on a series of trips that would be decisive for the future of his art. He went first of all to Algeria, where he discovered the light of northern Africa, and then to Italy, where he studied Raphael and the Pompeii frescoes. The Bérards welcomed him in Normandy at their château in Wargemont. He was received by Cézanne in L'Estaque, near Marseille. It was as much a discovery of new

Renoir devoted more and more time to family life after the birth of his first son, Pierre, in 1885. He began spending summers in Essoyes, in the village where Aline was born. The drawings and paintings executed at the time on the theme of maternity were also linked to memories of the works of Raphael which Renoir saw during his trip to Italy, a country where "each woman breast-feeding a child is one of Raphael's virgins!"

Madame Renoir et ses enfants. Paris, Bibliothèque Nationale.

places as of new cuisines. The countryfolk travelling by train were often loaded down with enough food for a trip around the world, and Renoir was frequently invited to partake in the feast. "As the miles went by, my father switched from the *gougère bourguignonne* to braised beef, from fresh young Côte d'Or wines to delicious rosés from the Rhone river valley," explained Jean.

As his feelings for Aline grew stronger, even to the point of obsession, Renoir finally renounced his adventuring life and his bachelorhood. The couple moved into a studio on the Rue Saint-Georges, but made the mistake of lodging with Madame Charigot during the first days. She had offered her skills as a cook, but it was a fatal error considering the domestic track record of the woman—she had driven her husband, an

*T*he painter Albert André, one of Renoir's closest friends near the end of his life, spent many summers at Essoyes. An attentive listener, he faithfully recorded his conversations with the master in a book published in 1919.

Renoir and Albert in Laudun in 1906.

upstanding winegrower of Essoyes, to flee the family home without warning, exiling himself as far away as North Dakota in the United States. Renoir most certainly enjoyed the soufflés, veal cutlets, clotted cream and the other delicious dishes prepared by his mother-in-law, but her constant wheedling—"Aren't you having any more veal? Some foie gras perhaps?"—would spoil the atmosphere considerably. If her son-in-law got up from the table during the meal to make a quick sketch, it would cause a scene; offended, the old woman would take her plate and go and eat alone next to the fireplace. To placate her mother, Aline knew of no better method than to run out and buy her a box of *marron glacés*.

When Pierre was born in 1885, a change was called for. With her usual sense of concern, Aline suggested that Renoir rent a studio away from the apartment, while she found another place where her mother could live. The birth would also cause a complete transformation of Renoir's life. "All the theories of new Athens were suddenly surpassed by the movement of a newborn's leg," said Jean. Although he didn't marry Aline until 1890, ten years after meeting her, with the baby's birth there was no longer any hiding their relationship from friends such as Berthe Morisot and Mallarmé.

During the fall of 1885, Renoir went to Essoyes for the first time. Aline rented a house on the outskirts of the village, on the Route de Loches, next to a mason. The back door opened on to the road leading to the Petit Clamart, a cluster of tall trees surrounded by a high wall in the middle of the field between the river and the hills. It was referred to by the locals as "The Clay Pot Hillside." During this first stay a portrait of Aline was painted in which she appears as a

country girl, simply dressed and wearing a straw hat decorated with roses. Renoir would keep this portrait until his death. Aline breastfeeding was the inspiration behind *L'Enfant au sein*, the archetypical image of rural maternity. It was a work by a proud father inspired by the Madonnas of the Renaissance he'd seen in Italy. Aline became the artist's favorite model. He would often sit down in the kitchen next to her to help with the meal, stopping after a few minutes to pull out a notebook and quickly scribble a sketch. Or else he would decide to draw live eels on the table, forcing Aline to abandon her idea of stewing them in wine for dinner. "With her natural instincts, she knew that Renoir was born to paint, just as grape vines were made to produce wine. It was therefore imperative that he paint, well or badly, with or without success, but

most importantly that he keep going," said Jean. Aline liked to watch him work, offering her opinion on a piece of work succinctly and in a straightforward manner. She wanted to remain exactly what she was, "a grape growers' daughter who knew how to bleed a chicken, wipe a baby's bottom, and clip the vines." Losing her accent was out of the question. Aline's kindness and simplicity made her very attractive. "Your wife is like a queen visiting a travelling circus," Degas remarked to Renoir one day at an exhibition opening at Durand-Ruel's gallery. Aline's love of good food and wine pleased Renoir in particular. The artist's lifestyle was essentially sober. He appreciated the good life and above all loved to find himself surrounded by people who liked to eat their fill. He was wary of those who didn't drink wine, "closet drunks," he would call them

in jest, just as he was mistrustful of those who didn't smoke. He was certain they had some kind of hidden vice. "It makes me happy to watch your mother eat," he would say to his son. "What a difference from the ladies of society who hold themselves back to stay thin and pale!"

Rather than play the role of "artist's wife" while in the company of Renoir's many guests and interfere with their interesting conversation, Aline preferred to busy herself by making the best meals possible. Although she stopped cooking them herself at a relatively young age, when Renoir's success allowed them to afford a cook, she carefully supervised all preparations. Madame Harigot and Marguerite Merlet, Renoir's mother, were her first cooking instructors. But Marie Corot was her true teacher. She was of no relation to the painter, but she'd been his cook during his childhood. She was a small, stout woman who always wore a blouse and a gray skirt, never an apron, and oversaw everything with "a seriousness possessed by a person who had prepared *gougères* for a famous painter, and was teaching the wife of another well-known painter how to thicken a sauce without adding flour," remembered Jean. Madame Renoir borrowed from her style of cooking, which was light, easy to prepare and without fuss, sometimes modifying certain of her recipes to her husband's taste. Sauces with flour, stock that had not been skimmed and food coloring were all prohibited. Not to overboil green vegetables was another of her staunch rules. Peas were cooked without a drop of water. In a cooking pot that wouldn't crack, she added several lettuce leaves that provided the necessary moisture. Rules for cooking times were strict. Housewives at the time were roasting meat for long periods of time. At the Renoir household,

*T*hadée Natanson, the founder of *La Revue Blanche*, gave a surprising description of Renoir: "His stride is speeded up by a sense of perpetual agitation which bends and straightens his back, and animates his tormented fingers. Even in his studio he wears a felt hat on his tiny head, which appears alive and greying, as if all his fever is concentrated . . . his deeply lined face is drawn and dry, covered in gray stubble, and above his prominent cheekbones, his eyes shine brightly."

Above: Renoir in 1885. Right: *Fraises*. Paris, Musée de l'Orangerie, Jean Walter-Paul Guillaume collection.

nothing was allowed to be overdone. Meat was cooked for twelve minutes per pound and not a minute more. Spit-roast meats were a favorite. A sheet-metal scallop was used for this, sitting upright in the fireplace, with a spit over the top turned by a spring system. The juice would then drip into the bottom of the scallop.

Renoir especially loved meat grilled in September on an open fire over a bed of blazing vine shoots. Thin pieces of meat were thrown on the dying coals, then pulled out and softened by being rubbed with butter, and served with no other seasoning. Renoir adored chestnuts and potatoes cooked on the open fire, as well as the regional cooking. Red beans with bacon, the *pièce de résistance* for the inhabitants of the Burgundy region, were a particular favorite with the painter. The wine growers in the area called the beans peas, and only ate those which grew in the vineyards. They turned their noses up at field beans, considered suitable only for workmen and pigs. Potatoes and large red plums were not regarded any better. Such culinary prejudice was not tolerated in the Renoir family. The painter made it clear to his sons that one must not dislike "regular food." "If one of us refused to eat our beans, you could be sure that he or she would be eating beans and nothing else until we decided to like them wholeheartedly," remembered Jean.

Watching bread being made was another treat. The dough was pulled out of the large carved oak kneading-trough that was kept in the living room and baked in a stone oven. When the stones inside turned bright red, the coals were pushed back into the corner with a sort of toothless rake. In would go whatever was to be cooked: loaves of brown bread; back of pork; enormous fruit tarts with cherries, plums, greengages, blackcurrants, grapes or wild apples, depending on the season. Renoir preferred these

In 1895, on Aline's advice, Renoir bought a house in Essoyes where he would henceforth spend his summers. He was visited by many friends, including George Rivière, Ambroise Vollard and Paul Cézanne. Renoir fell in love with the place and built a studio at the end of his garden. His youngest son Claude, nicknamed Coco, was born here in 1901. Away from the city, Renoir rediscovered his taste for the simpler things in life, and was quickly adopted by the inhabitants of the village.

La Maison de Renoir vue du Jardin. Private collection.

homemade desserts to the "magnificent fare showcased in Parisian shop windows." He felt the same way about Essoyes wine, poured into pitchers in the stone caves. It was a wine without a trace of sugar, which he considered highly superior to the mix of wines served in the French capital. He also disliked the heavy taste of aged wines. "One must sample, not drink. It becomes ceremonious. One even behaves as if it were the elevation of the Host," he said jokingly. He made fun of the mannerisms of the "connoisseurs who rinse their gums as though with a mouthwash, raising their eyes to the sky in ecstasy." Renoir was much happier in the company of the local winegrowers, whom he found "generous," and less inclined to deny themselves pleasure than the farmers. He felt they knew how to appreciate a good supper after returning home from the vineyards, deriving much more pleasure out of life. Renoir wasn't a heavy drinker, but he learned

how to guess the origin of a wine after spending many hours with the winegrowers. He could identify the "Pinot of the Larpin vineyard," the best in the area. He loved to listen to the people of Essoyes compare the qualities of the different types of soil: one which gave a taste of gunflint, another of more clay-like texture that gave the wine a full-bodied taste, and yet another that offered a good bouquet. Despite his silent nature and his Parisian accent, Renoir was quickly adopted by the local people. "He didn't talk politics, his ties weren't in fashion, but the locals loved him anyway," said Gabrielle. "Even the suspicious and unfriendly Bataillé mother allowed him to paint her children."

When he set up his painting stool in front of his house to paint the village road and the church bells that could be seen above the tree-tops, the neighbor's children would creep up timidly, whispering "Look, the painter!" or a vineyard

worker pushing a cart would stop and strike up a conversation. But those who complained of a poor harvest had to be careful. Renoir would launch into a speech in support of country life that Georges Rivière would write about in his biography: "How can you complain when you have everything a reasonable man could want to be happy. . . . Your pantry is full, and you have a relative or a friend to share a bottle of wine with. You work, but your job is nothing like those who work in the city. You live in the outdoors and you work more or less when you want to. And you have freedom, real freedom, because you don't depend on anyone but yourself and you are the master of your own house. What more could you want to be happy?"

The summers in Essoyes were among the happiest moments in Renoir's life. Every time he

arrived he would throw a party to celebrate "living the country life in Champagne, escaping the expensive models of Paris to paint laundresses and washerwomen at the river's edge." The family would leave Paris in early July. First they boarded a train to Troyes, then took a second train to Polisot. It was quite a chaotic trip considering everything they had to carry with them: easels, canvases and umbrellas, as well as suitcases belonging to Renoir, Aline and the faithful model Gabrielle, with the two children, Pierre and Jean, in tow. When they arrived at Polisot, they were greeted by Fluteau the innkeeper who would assume the role of coachman, and by Clément Mugnier, a cousin of Aline who looked after the house and kept the garden in order while the Renoirs were in Paris. Lively and natural, generous and devoted as well as having a healthy appetite, Clément shared Renoir's love of mankind and his unlimited sense of optimism. The carriage was pulled by Coco, a nickname that most people in Burgundy had the habit of giving their horses. Several miles before they arrived at the village, the landscape would begin to change. Vineyards replaced the fields, known as fallow lands by the residents of Essoyes—plateaus covered with flat rocks where the farmers used to build their huts, shacks that remained cool in the summer and in which they stored their tools and took shelter during the cold months.

The village of Essoyes was further ahead. In 1895, at Aline's insistence, Renoir bought a house at the edge of the village. It was in the upper part of Essoyes, generally home to the winegrowers of the area, while the local farmers lived in lower Essoyes. Renoir's house was a solid rural structure in the rough stone that he was so fond of, with a small vineyard and several fruit trees in the back garden. Several years later he bought a semi-detached house, working in two of the rooms on the first floor while a real studio was built at the back of the garden. These additions allowed Aline to fix up extra rooms for the many guests from Paris who would arrive to stay. A billiard room was also built.

The house was sparsely decorated and the furniture consisted of several country antiques. Renoir despised rosewood furniture, and in general disliked any kind that was manufactured in bulk, lacking the "made-by-hand" feel. He had a fondness for the era when a carpenter created his own designs, putting his whole heart into their construction. Renoir often spoke out strongly against the industrial age. Straight back chairs and Thonet armchairs produced in Austria were the only few manufactured objects in the

house that met with his approval. Display cabinets and knick-knacks from Meissen or Sèvres were also banned from his home, but huge bouquets of roses in inexpensive vases decorated by hand which Aline found in the market were accepted. Bolts of brightly colored calico adorned the windows, while numerous paintings, most of them without frames, hung on the walls. There were one or two old frames, bought from antique dealers, and frames from the previous century decorated with designs chiselled in the hard wood, which Renoir approved of and even had gilded with gold leaf. The table had no displays of silverware or glasses. "A pile of forks, knives

"*The* best thing for a woman to do is to bend down and clean the floor, light the fire, or do the washing, as this kind of movement is good for her stomach," said Renoir.

Les Laveuses. The Baltimore Museum of Art, the Cone Collection formed by Dr. Claribel Cone and Miss Etta Cone of Baltimore, Maryland.

and glasses of all shapes and sizes just to swallow a soft-boiled egg washed down with a glass of cheap wine," he would grumble. However, Renoir felt strongly about having silver knives rather than metal for cutting fruit.

In general, Renoir abhorred all that was imitation. That judgement was applied to everything from waxed cloth used instead of a real tablecloth to salts put in jugs of tap water to make it look like Vichy water. He considered cut crystal bottles to be vulgar and preferred the straightforward bottles made in Bar-sur-Seine that were handmade and irregular in shape, with the chunky glass giving off greenish reflections of light. As he was terrified his children would injure themselves on the sharp edges of the furniture and mantelpieces he broke off the corners of the marble table, sanding them smooth with sandpaper. For the same safety reasons, he had the floorboards washed with water and refused to have them waxed. There was also no bleach about, in case the children should swallow it. He required Gabrielle to keep all cleaning products and pharmaceutical goods well out of arm's reach in the kitchen. He had a difficult battle on his hands when he wanted the brass

polished, having to convince her that chimney ash really was more effective than chemical-based products. If the family cook made the fatal mistake of using an enamel utensil to prepare the meals, she would once again have to endure the story of Renoir's misadventure during a lunch with Paul Gallimard in a fancy hotel in Nice when a sharp piece of enamel was found sticking out of his fried eggs.

Gabrielle would rise at 6 a.m., calling upon Marie Corot or another local woman to help her. Renoir would breakfast alone in the dining room, enjoying a cup of *café au lait*, in which he would dunk pieces of bread that were toasted in the fireplace and spread with a layer of fresh butter. It was always served in slabs, as Renoir turned his nose up at small squares or sculpted pieces of butter. As Aline and the children got up and the servants, guests and visiting models began to stir, the house would come alive. Days were structured around long family walks in the woods or along the edge of the Ource, a tributary of the Seine that ran through the lower part of the village. Another destination was Verpillières, a village nearly two miles away from Essoyes, to see the Roman church with an enormous elm in front that was said to have been planted in the days of Joan of Arc.

After they returned from their walk, the Renoirs would often visit Aline's cousins. One of them, Cedrine, would frequently prepare a dinner of "soaked bread," warming up old wine mixed with sugar and serving it with toast. Then there was Victor, Renoir's older brother, whom Aline helped find a place to live in Essoyes. Another regular was the gardener Aubert, the only person in Essoyes to grow melons, green beans and peas in his garden on the edge of the Ource river. Alternatively, they would dine at Gabrielle's

*I*n directing his film *Une partie de campagne,* which was based on Maupassant's work, Jean Renoir undoubtedly relived the many family picnics during their stays at Essoyes: what a pleasure it was to stretch out on the grass with a full stomach, having enjoyed stuffed pigeon and a Japanese salad (photographs opposite and recipes pages 166 and 144), washed down with a good local wine.

father's house, where, before fighting over the boar's head, the story about the young wild boar that was given to Gabrielle would be told again. When the animal grew into an enormous fully grown boar and nearly slit the throat of a cow he was eventually reduced to ham and sausage. Another time, a meal was shared at Aline's cousins' home to celebrate a baptism. It was a five-hour affair, served on trestles set up in a barn, with natural-colored sheeting draped on the walls and roses inserted into the material. Jean Renoir, who was chosen as the godfather, remembered the day well: "We poured a drink for the new Christian. My father was insistent that we put a bit of water in the wine. The mother of the child gave in to his strange request, but didn't let her daughter know. The glass of lightly baptized liquid was given to my niece. She tasted it, made a face, and said: 'I don't like water.'"

It was during the wine harvest in October that the number of family gatherings increased. Aline would take the boys to their cousins' home, and each one, with a basket strapped on his back,

would cut grapes with a real pruning knife, then carefully pour his load in the "sink," and watch every stage of the operation, from pressing the grapes to tasting the sweet wines. The barn where the wood casks for fermenting the wine were kept was a mysterious place for the children, who were frightened of the moving shadows and the echoing voices.

Every summer the house would be invaded by friends. Some would be regulars like Georges Rivière and his two daughters Hélène and Renée, the future wives of Edmond Renoir and Paul Cézanne, the son of the painter. Renée had a wonderful voice (Renoir would often ask her to sing) but was also quite naive, which made her a perfect target for the children. Playing blind man's bluff in the middle of a herd of cows at a neighbor's farm, she would have her eyes blindfolded and then be left alone amongst the placid creatures. It was a joke that was repeated over and over, and resulted in the children receiving a sound whipping with a switch of hazel. The art dealers Georges Durand-Ruel and

During picnics by the river, the Renoir family avoided sitting near the ponds where it seemed even cows could disappear. Servigny was Renoir's favorite spot. There were plenty of springs, a majestic avenue of poplars, and an ancient castle where only a few sections of wall survived.

Ambroise Vollard, Julie Manet, Albert Faivre and the painter Albert André and his wife Maleck would also spend many summers in Essoyes. The sculptor Maillol came on one occasion and sculpted a bust of Renoir in his studio, while the painter worked away on his own projects.

Some days the coach was hitched up, while on others the bicycles were taken out. More and more of Renoir's friends were using this form of transport, and in the end the artist gave in and used a bicycle himself. When he was by himself he rode it to look for subject material, making rough sketches in his notebook, as his painting gear was far too cumbersome to carry out into the countryside.

"Renoir's gang" sometimes went to Riceys on the Laigne river, the land of rosé wine some 19 miles from Essoyes. After admiring the village and the château that overlooked the river, they would eat in an old inn. Sitting next to the huge fireplace, they would tuck into a casserole of chicken and "green beans with grelons," also

known as beans with bacon, accompanied by several glasses of rosé wine.

When he stayed at home to work in his studio at the base of the garden the children were warned not to disturb him, but he loved hearing the sounds of their laughter and game-playing. One of his favorite places for painting outdoor portraits was a grassy corner in front of the studio, where an old crooked apple tree stood. The light diffused by the leaves of the trees was perfect for Renoir. This is where he posed Aline, one of his three sons (Claude was born in Essoyes in 1901), Gabrielle, who was dragged away from her household chores, and the model who came down every year from Paris. There was also Georgette Pigeot, a beautiful blonde with a clear complexion, who during her modelling sessions would tell amusing stories or put on false airs. There was also Adrienne, another beautiful blonde with a regal walk, who before her marriage had an affair with a baker boy working at a bakery on the Rue de Chaussée d'Antin,

where Renoir would buy his rye bread. "In addition to her skill of sitting brilliantly, she also had the God-given gift of being able to cook *pomme frîtes* no less divinely," wrote Jean Renoir.

This was an unusual household, where the cooks had to have "skin that wouldn't reflect light," and the models, florists, dressmakers, and apprentices imitated the style of Molière's servants, and helped out at the stove after their modelling session. Once the sun was too low in the sky, Renoir would put down his paint brushes, methodically clean his palette and go in to sit beside the fireplace, where all the cooking was done. "In the corner the food was cooking on the open fire, in another corner the house girl was heating irons. In the middle, hanging on a hook above the fire, the soup simmered in a huge cast-iron pot," said Jean. After dinner, the guests

would sit around the piano and Renée Rivière would play an aria by Mozart. When the guests had departed, Renoir would sit on a bench in the dining room and listen to his cousin Clément's comments on the farmers returning from their fields, smiling at his jibe, "Well, what do you expect, you're from the city," aimed at Aline, who was always outraged by his saucy jokes.

The return trips to Paris were melancholy affairs. To make the transition from Essoyes to the city less brutal and to retain the sensations of the country a little longer, the Renoir family would board a train carrying copious amounts of food, including a ham smoked in the fireplace, and bottles of *marc*.

The Ource, a tributary of the Seine, ran below the village of Essoyes. One of the painter's favorite settings was near the Loches bridge. The river flowed over stones, the grass rippled in the breeze. Renoir compared these colors to "molten silver." Jean laid down nets to catch fish while Aline fished with a pole, filling the basket with minnows and tiny fish which Marie Corot, the cook, deep fried in oil from the wild flowers: "Seeds which gave yellow flowers that invaded the fields," remembered Jean.

Étude de torse, effets de soleil. Paris, Musée d'Orsay.

89

At Les Collettes

*"We're up to our necks in seeds, just like the
old man in La Fontaine's Fables. The peas are
doing well, and the potatoes are not doing
badly either. For the moment, we are
swimming in happiness . . ."*

A letter from Renoir

Baptistin pushed Renoir's wheelchair, Aline laid a woolen blanket over her husband's lap, Gabrielle carried the basket containing the lunch which Old Louise had prepared: Renoir was going to Les Collettes to paint. The artist had spent every winter since 1903 at Cagnes, in the old post office. During this time, the property at Les Collettes with its twisted olive trees and little farmhouse with its red-orange tile roof never failed to inspire him. As soon as the warm weather arrived the ever-faithful Baptistin, who had been a hackney cab driver before coming to work for the family, harnessed the horses to the carriage and drove "the boss" over to the property, situated opposite the village on the other side of the valley.

Adorned with a white parasol, the carriage wended its way among the orange orchards that covered the hillsides. Zaza, the family dog, followed behind, overjoyed at the prospect of digging up the bone which she had buried at the foot of an olive tree the previous week.

Living at Les Colettes at the time were an Italian peasant, Paul Canova, his mother

The olive trees that lined the hills of Les Collettes were an inspiration to Renoir. "Five centuries of existence, through storms and droughts, hurricanes and frosts, pruning and neglect, gave them the most unexpected forms. Some of the trunks looked like barbaric divinities. Branches were twisted around each other, forming patterns the most daring designer wouldn't have come up with," said Jean.

Paysage des Collettes. Cagnes, Musée des Collettes.

91

*R*enoir visited the south of France for the first time in 1880 in the company of Claude Monet. He was filled with enthusiasm for the intensity of the colors and light on the Cote d'Azur, and the climate was beneficial to his rheumatism. From 1897 onwards he spent nearly every winter here. Before moving to Cagnes, he lived in the village of Magagnosc, in Cannet, and in Nice.

From left to right: the painters Valtat, d'Espagnat and Renoir at Magagnosc, near Grasse, around 1900–1901.

Catherine and a mule called Litchou. Old Catherine had a reputation in the region of being a witch, and her curses were feared. She understood the properties of herbs and healed wounds with spider's webs, utilizing the penicillin they contained without knowing it.

Seated in the carriage, Renoir looked for a landscape to paint. He finally chose the village of Cagnes, visible among the the olive trees. The village, with its narrow cobblestone streets, was dominated by a castle that had once belonged to the Grimaldis, which an eccentric Russian woman, Madame Carbonel, was restoring. It had previously been used as a storage space by the fire brigade, and before that as a stable.

Singing softly to himself, Renoir stood blinking in the sun in front of his canvas, which was protected from the glare by a parasol. The trees' golden leaves allowed just enough of the sun's rays through to draw arabesques of light on the tall, dense grass, strewn with pretty wildflowers. His white canvas hat was pushed far back on his head. Renoir feared not so much sunstroke as the effect of the sun's rays on the brain, "the seat of perception and discernment of detail," which he believed to be at the rear of the skull. He thought that by exposing it to ultraviolet rays one ran the risk not of losing one's senses but, much more seriously, of no longer being able to distinguish between one shade of gray and another. It was all right to go about with one's head uncovered, he said, if one wanted to be a Michelet or a Pasteur, but if one aspired to be a Rubens it was better to wear a hat.

On this particular day a despondent Paul Canova came looking for Renoir, not to admire his painting (in which he was only slightly interested) but to announce that an estate agent from Nice was seeking to buy Les Collettes with the intention of cutting down the trees and moving a horticulturist into the farmhouse to grow carnations. Canova's mother was beside herself, and was threatening to hole herself up in the house in protest.

While he listened to this news, Renoir cast his dreamy gaze over several hundred-year-old olive trees (planted, so the story went, by the soldiers of François I as a way of keeping them busy during a ceasefire in the war against Charles V). Sculpted by storms and drought, they had grown unchecked throughout the years. Their twisted branches wrapped round one another in barbarous forms, lending them a rare majesty and a certain airy lightness. The very thought of

seeing these beautiful old trees turned into napkin rings inscribed with the words "Souvenir from Nice" was intolerable.

Assisted by Paul, Renoir climbed back into the carriage and asked Baptistin to drive him back to his wife. Aline, summoned by her husband, interrupted a card game to see the landlady, Madame Armand, immediately to try to prevent the massacre.

The Renoirs bought the land on 28 June 1907. Madame Armand was pleased to see her property go to Renoir, saying to Monsieur Barbarin, the notary, "At least we know this lot!"

Had Renoir been alone he would perhaps have been happy just to convert the old farmhouse, but not wanting to deprive the Canovas of a home, and to please Aline, who was tired of moving, he decided to build a house on the land.

The site chosen for the house turned out to be very near the farmhouse—not for want of space, as the new owners had six acres to choose from, but because the situation offered a splendid view of the sea. The construction had its problems. The architect wished to build a pretentious villa like those that littered the coast at the time, while the artist wanted a simple building that would harmonize with the surrounding countryside. Long discussions took place to ensure that the house would have a northern exposure in order to gain the best light, a principle that the unfortunate architect seemed incapable of understanding. Renoir did drawings for him and explained it calmly so as not to upset him, but once he had gone the painter would give vent to his anger.

Renoir had often teased his friends when they boasted of the remoteness of their homes. "Why not live in a cemetery? Mind you, even there you would have visitors!" In order to compensate for

*R*enoir conserved the rustic nature of Les Collettes, with its old tiled farmhouse and olive trees. Aline insisted that a new building be constructed, one that would be large enough for the painter to receive his friends. It was built by a Nice architect in an open field at the top of the hill. Finished in 1908, it had every modern comfort: running water, electricity, central heating and a telephone.

Right: Brouillade aux legumes, see recipe page 174.

the isolation of Les Collettes, he wanted the house to be large and comfortable enough to receive many friends. It was a way of providing a link with the convivial atmosphere of the Château des Brouillards, his Paris residence—the difference being that Rivière, Vollard, the Durand-Ruels and Maurice Gangnat would have to journey fifteen hours by train to visit him, as opposed to the few minutes necessary to take the tram to Montmartre.

The autumn of 1908 was a magical time for the Renoirs as they took possession of their new home. It was the meeting of two worlds: a house without a past and a family who brought with them their history, their dreams, their gaiety, and their colors. The wicker baskets which Baptistin unloaded from the cart were overflowing with dishes, linens and children's toys.

Old Louise hurried into her first-floor kitchen, her baskets flowing over with a veritable harvest of fresh vegetables, painstakingly selected at the market. For the evening meal she prepared a cod stew served with potatoes, with a pinenut pie for dessert. Singing the whole while, she stowed away her pots and saucepans in the kitchen, the centerpiece of which was a brand new wood-burning stove.

Aline, who only ever seemed really happy in the country, lost no time in indulging her passion for gardening as soon as the house was finished. She had already made plans for a vegetable garden and a henhouse.

Jean moved into his second-floor bedroom. Keen on reptiles, he had a good laugh at a model's screams when, delivering a pile of sheets, she discovered the huge lizards which he kept in a glass cage in his room.

For Aline, this first day was a triumph. She finally had a vast house, with all the modern conveniences: electricity, running water, a telephone and central heating.

At first disappointed with the house's austere proportions, Renoir was pleased to discover a superb view of the Cap d'Antibes from his room.

Less profoundly Mediterranean than Cézanne, less sensitive to the passionate violence of Provence than Van Gogh, Renoir was nevertheless bewitched by the countryside and its abundant vegetation: shiny-leaved orange trees, ancient olive trees with knotty trunks, and a multi-colored profusion of wildflowers. "In this marvellous place it feels as though no misfortune can touch you, and you live in a cocoon," he would later remark.

A large avenue wound in a semi-circle around the orange orchards, leading to the house, set in a slightly somber courtyard. The trees bent slowly in the breeze, mop-head hydrangeas flourished next to the oleanders, the dogs stretched out asleep in the grass: such was Renoir's estate.

Inside the house, the light-colored walls and ceiling lent an atmosphere of sweet harmony. The

During Renoir's lifetime, Les Collettes was self-sufficient. With the help of two assistants, Aline looked after the vegetable garden that contained a vast field of artichokes, patches of green salads, cabbage, lima beans and green beans, as well as a large section of red-skinned potatoes. Dill, borage, thyme and other herbs gave flavor to the Provençal dishes of Old Louise, the cook. The produce from the gardens was stored during the winter or sold at the market.

man who lived here was successful, his paintings selling for higher and higher prices. The desire for a calm working place was the inspiration behind this place. Apart from the family's and the servants' quarters, the second floor comprised two studios, only one of which was originally intended for this purpose. Right from the very first winter at Les Collettes, the radiator in the large studio proved insufficient to heat it. In spite of setting up the good old ceramic stove which he'd had for years, Renoir was forced to move into a nearby, smaller room.

The living room was on the first floor. A stone-tiled floor added freshness to this dimly-lit room, furnished with chairs covered in a rose-patterned fabric that matched the wallpaper.

Next door was the dining room, fitted with large French doors. This was the painter's favorite place. At sunset, he would ask to be carried in and placed in front of the fireplace, built according to his own design. On this same floor were the bedrooms reserved for his closest friends: the Durand-Ruels, Gangnat, Albert André, or the children of departed friends such as Marie and Pierre Lestringuez.

In this vast dwelling, filled with children's laughter and women's voices, each element had been chosen for its craftsmanship, its past or its aesthetic appeal, and always for its simplicity. For Renoir could have adopted this motto of interior decorating: "The charm of imperfection is preferable to imperfection without charm."

"*P*arisians' love of olive oil, bouillabaisse, sea urchins, and *brandade* is relatively new. When I was young, we all ate in the style of the south. I've said before that Renoir felt that a painting was most beautiful in the area in which it was painted. His reasoning was also applied to life in general, and eating in particular," said Jean Renoir.

Left: Bouillabaisse d'Aline, see recipe page 152.

103

In the dining room hung a portrait of Madame Colonna-Romano, a member of the Comédie Française, painted by Renoir around 1910. He had just earned international fame, and thanks to the dealer Durand-Ruel his paintings were being shown all over Europe and the United States. Many famous people at the time were commissioning portraits from him.

Portrait de Madame Colonna-Romano. Cagnes-sur-Mer, Musée des Collettes. Right: Tarte aux figues, see recipe page 177.

A throng of visitors descended on Les Collettes. "The boss is at work! Leave him in peace!" Gabrielle would chastize them. Sometimes Renoir would receive them politely, sometimes with amusement. Other times, irritated, he would shut himself away, speaking to no one and behaving in a perfectly horrible manner to all. He was never to get used to the trappings of celebrity, to all the requests, some flattering, others devious or tiresome, which make up the daily lot of a famous painter. The visits of his fellow artists were no exception. Matisse admired Renoir. From the moment of his arrival in Nice he came immediately to Les Collettes, where the master received him cordially. After having cast a disapproving glance at some of Matisse's canvases, he said to him, "In all honesty, I don't like your work. I would like to tell you that you are not a good painter, or even that you are a very bad painter, but one thing prevents me from doing so: when you place a black spot on your canvas, it stays where it is put."

At the request of the dealer Bernheim, Auguste Rodin came to Les Collettes in January 1914 so that Renoir could do a portrait of him in red chalk. But the visit was brief: Rodin's insolent disposition annoyed Renoir, and the day of his departure was one of relief for the entire household.

The visitors were not all undesirable; some of the admirers who made their pilgrimages to Les Collettes had travelled long distances with little money, and their journeys had been arduous and difficult. The ever-generous Aline would lead them into the dining room, where Old Louise would feed them. Then, Renoir, notified of their arrival, would invite them into the studio. They would spend long, fulfilling moments silently

admiring the painter as he laid paint upon the canvas with his deformed fingers gripping the brush.

Some of the more brave would try to understand his secrets, to analyze the composition of his palette; to them he would answer, "All that is chemistry, not painting. If one could explain a painting, it would no longer be art. Being indescribable and inimitable are two qualities which make up a work of art."

Les Collettes was the perfect setting for Renoir's last period; in his studio at Cagnes he painted *Les Grandes Baigneuses*, which he considered to be the crowning point of his career.

Aline's Gardens

With the help of Paul Canova and his mother, Aline had been ceaselessly working on the grounds of the estate since the family had moved in. Behind the farmhouse, she planted fruit trees on the terraces which were held up by small stone walls. The bounty from the vegetable garden not only supplied the family's daily food but also served as models for several of Renoir's still-lifes. Around the house, where clumps of pines and Canary Island palms were already growing, she added blue-leaved, odorous eucalyptus. Long beds of blue irises lined the lawns. Wishing to keep his "earthly paradise" intact, Renoir did not hesitate to replace a row of orange trees, a favorite target of children, with ones of the Seville variety, the fruit of which is bitter and inedible.

Other plantings were carried out on a grand scale. Orange flower blossoms were harvested in the springtime with the help of young girls from the village. On these days there were endless comings and goings, with laughter and singing

On the mantelpiece of the living room sat a clay bust of Coco, the youngest son, sculpted by Renoir. The painter's hands, deformed by rheumatism, could no longer grasp anything, and so he gave direction with a long stick to the young Catalan sculptor Richard Guino. In a vase stood a bouquet of wild flowers. Renoir especially loved daisies and poppies.

Left: Coco and his friends at Les Collettes around 1908. Opposite: Mado Enspach (the wife of a writer friend of Renoir and Cézanne) and Malek and Albert André around the table at Renoir's home at Les Collettes in Cagnes in 1917.

among the rows of trees. Renoir, delighted at the spectacle, allowed himself to become tipsy in the shade of the lime trees, intoxicated by the enchanting perfume from these delicate, white blossoms which filled their baskets.

In the winter, the young from the village took the route which led to Les Collettes for the harvesting of olives. Large tarpaulins were spread out on the ground and the girls would beat the branches with long poles, causing the ripe fruit to fall. Once loaded up, the wagons left for the mill at Béal. After a long wait the first-pressed oil, called "la fleur," collected in large, clay jars, was quickly taken back to Les Collettes. In the dining room, in front of the fire, Renoir awaited the rite of the "roustide," in which the entire family took part. This consisted of taking a piece of bread toasted over the fire, rubbing it with garlic and

When Renoir bought Les Collettes, the old house that had charmed him, an old Italian countrywoman lived there. Catherine Canova and her son Paul had looked after the place poorly. The red-orange roof tiles, the peeling walls, the wood balcony and the faded olive green shutters of the house appeared in many of Renoir's paintings, as the artist preserved the building's decayed charm. Along the walls ran a blue-flowered La Paz tomato plant and date plants. In front of the farmhouse stood an olive tree with a knotted trunk.

pouring a thin stream of the "fleur" over it—the golden, shining and transparent oil. "A treat for the gods!" Renoir would exclaim.

As a true daughter of winegrowers, Aline planted vines all along the terraces. While they did not produce good wines, they did give an excellent crop of grapes. She also built greenhouses in which she grew winter crops of carnations and roses. She then composed magnificent bouquets which were placed throughout the house to provide a constant source of inspiration for Renoir.

The vegetable plot was at the bottom of the garden, near the farmouse. There, Aline cultivated vegetables and herbs—the wild thyme, basil and savory that went into her recipes. For the Renoirs, there was nothing finer than radishes or tomatoes freshly picked from the garden. Aline tended her garden as if she were taking part in a sacred rite; there was no question of cutting a head of lettuce that had not achieved the proper size, or of picking a tomato that was not quite ripe.

In between the farmhouse and the vegetable garden were the toolsheds and the storage places for the compost heaps and the tinned winter preserves. Hidden behind the farmhouse were the goat pens, the hen house, the rabbit hutch, and a wood stove where breads and pies were baked, all contributing to a life of complete independence at Les Collettes.

Renoir left Aline to direct the planting as she saw fit, but none the less no detail escaped his attention. One day, when a workman toiling in the garden offered to pull up some weeds, he demanded to know, "What weeds are those?" Unlike his friend Claude Monet, for whom a garden was the end result of much solitary contemplation and planning, Renoir prided

*I*n the south, Renoir felt protected from the troubles of the world. "In this marvellous place," he said one day to his friend Rivière, "it feels as though no misfortune can touch you, and that you live in a cocoon."

Right (above): *La Ferme des Collettes*. Cagnes-sur-Mer, Musée des Collettes.

Right (below): Renoir, his wife and their son Claude, in Cannet in 1902.

himself in preserving the wildness of Les Collettes, much preferring the untamed weeds to a tailored lawn.

The Cooking Lessons of Dinan

"We surprised everyone by eating in the fashion of the Midi."—Jean Renoir

Behind the walls at Les Collettes, cooking was a separate art, where earth and sky breathed out the enticing odors of the Midi.

Renoir believed that a painting was most beautiful in the place where it was painted. He applied the same reasoning to the art of living in general, and in particular to eating. He approved of the people of the South closing their shutters in the summer, not going out in the sun without a hat, and putting garlic in everything they ate. Under the Midi sun the artist lived as a southerner, but back in Montmartre he quickly reverted to the lifestyle of a Parisian.

Renoir surprised visitors to Les Collettes by serving them regional dishes, which were

generally considered exotic but none the less appreciated for their flavors. Renoir was much amused by his friend Georges Rivière who, although claiming to hate garlic, accepted several helpings of Madame Renoir's bouillabaisse, without realizing that it contained immoderate portions of it.

The cook at Les Collettes was none other than Ferdinand Isnard (known as Dinan), the owner of the old post office where the Renoirs had stayed before moving to Les Collettes. This jovial man, a chef by trade, was once a member of the famous team under the great Escoffier. After a glorious career, culminating at the Savoy in London, he had retired to Cagnes.

Having bought a rabbit or a thrush from the local poachers he would make his triumphal entry at Les Collettes, announcing, "Monsieur Renoir, I'm going to make you a good stew!" or even, "How do you want the thrush, with or without herbs?" Renoir normally detested interruptions while he was working, but these questions of Dinan's didn't disturb him. "With the others all is lost, but with him everything stays in my head and even becomes clarified," he said. Sometimes Dinan approached Madame Renoir or even Gabrielle to find out what would best please "the boss" that day: "Do you think he would enjoy braised beef?"

As soon as he began work at the stove this normally gentle man would be transformed into a veritable dictator, handing out orders succinctly and precisely. Gabrielle peeled the carrots, Old Louise cut up the meat, listening to the great chef's advice, and Jean stoked the fire while Madame Renoir carefully wrote down the recipe. The secret of his success lay in slow cooking over a gentle and regular heat, for he felt one should be able to eat a good braised beef with

a spoon and no knife, with the meat simply melting in the mouth.

Renoir, who never painted by artificial light, had already left his studio. Seated in front of the fireplace, where a wood fire crackled, he awaited with pleasurable anticipation the beef that had been stewing for six long hours, and whose wonderful aroma had already pervaded the entire house. The mood of the chef finally calmed when he brought the dish out to the dining room. He took a place at the table next to Renoir, so he could select the very best morsels for him. The whole family savored the delight of eating Dinan's succulent beef.

Dinan never used his *haute cuisine* recipes. "Leave that for the customers at the Savoy! Except that I once made cod with cream for the Prince of Wales; he loved it."

Renoir bought the land around Les Collettes to save the orchards of olive trees that were to be pulled down. In his landscapes, he used the panorama of the hillside and old Cagnes as subjects. Alternatively, he painted the old farmhouse and its ancient and twisted olive trees, with their silver leaves and roots resembling hardened lava. "Look at the light of the olive trees . . ." he would say, "they shine like diamonds . . . they're pink, and blue . . . and the sky behind . . . it's enough to drive you mad! The shadows of the olive trees are often purple; they are always moving, full of light, merriment and life.."

Left: Renoir and Claude as a child at the villa.
Printemps: Le Cannet, 1902.

*O*utdoor or indoor swimmers were one of Renoir's favorite subjects at the end of his life, his ideal of the female form being full-figured, closely approaching those preferred by Rubens. Here, the swimmer is ignoring the viewer. The innocence of the nymph is accentuated by the fact that the painter selected a very young model. "The simplest subjects are eternal; the naked woman coming out of the water or her bed is called Venus, or Nini. Nothing better can be invented," said Renoir to the painter Albert André.

Baigneuse aux cheveux longs. Paris, Musée de l'Orangerie, Jean Walter-Paul Guillaume collection.

Aline made sure that Dinan's recipes were followed closely. It must be said that she was under good guidance with the old chef. He taught her to make succulent jams with vegetables from the garden. Every season, whole crates of them filled the kitchen. Maximum effort was expended on the choosing, sniffing, peeling, shelling, sugaring, cooking . . . a thousand verbs and as many gestures at which the models and the servants excelled, all under the direction of Dinan and the watchful eye of Madame Renoir. Days were also spent preparing and sterilizing the preserves which were then placed in storage, safe from light. Aline filled jars which were carefully lined along the shelves, while Coco and his brothers, just like the greedy characters they were, set about creating chaos.

As much influence as Dinan had in Madame Renoir's kitchen, it was not to him but to the mayor of the nearby village of l'Estaque that she owed one of her greatest masterpieces: the bouillabaisse.

Her secret? Small coastal fish, sautéed in olive oil with onions and tomatoes. Then hot water and lots of garlic and herbs. The large fish and the shellfish were put in to poach when the base was ready. Finally, the scorpion fish and the saffron were added at the very end of the cooking time. The soup, passed through a sieve, was then poured over slices of toasted bread that had been rubbed with garlic. Aline's bouillabaisse was a favorite with Renoir's friends. The wife of the painter Caillebotte once said, " I have a chef who has cooked for the Prince of Wales, and who knows all the writings on cuisine by heart. Madame Renoir gives a few vague instructions to one of her husband's models who supervises the cooking in between sittings—my bouillabaisse is inedible, and hers is a marvel!"

The Children's Tea

Coco amused himself watching troops of ants carrying breadcrumbs across the white tablecloth. Jean was feeding his lizard, which liked to keep warm beneath his jacket.

It was four-thirty in the afternoon. Beneath the spreading lime tree, Gabrielle laid a small table for the children's tea, which was often a moment of respite from a game of hide-and-seek or another attack on the olive trees in the garden. Old Louise prepared apple and dough fritters, still warm and flavored with orange flower water. With help from Baptistin, she carefully carried Renoir, on his stretcher, into the garden, choosing a warm spot in which to place him. Gabrielle cried out, "Look, sir, I've found an olive!"

"Gabrielle, you know very well there are no olives at this time of year. It must be a goat turd!" When the children came close enough to his paint brush, he would tickle their noses. Renoir was overflowing with affection for his children. Aged and sickly, he found the strength and health in his offspring which were lacking in his body. When they were young, Renoir didn't want their hair to be cut. His refusal stemmed not only from his painter's taste for long, flowing, golden hair, but also from his personal theory on childhood: "The hair gives protection from falls and bumps, not to mention the dangers of the sun. If we remove natural defenses from children we will have to watch over them all the time, which is a way of curbing their spirit." Jean, who had a rather temperamental character, still had long golden locks at age seven, making him look like a little girl. He hated them so much he wanted to be bald. Coco, the youngest son, was one of Renoir's favorite models at Les Collettes and was immortalized in the *Clown rouge*. During the sittings, Renoir allowed the child to move about as he pleased. When a detail in the painting required that he sit still, Gabrielle would read him a children's story, which entertained Renoir as much as it did the child. Their favorite stories were Shishkabob Soup and the Brave Wooden Soldier, which they came to know by heart. Coco was never punished for being naughty during a sitting. When even Hans Andersen's tales could not make him sit still Renoir would send him away, saying, "Don't say anything. He might start hating the studio!"

Renoir dreamt of seeing his children work with ceramics. He set aside a corner of his studio just for them. This father, hostile to all forms of restraint, sought to form their tastes in this way, giving free reign to their imaginations. In the silence of the studio, Renoir enjoyed their seriousness as they worked the clay with touches of paint applied with hesitation but determination. The pieces were then taken to the furnace in the garden. Keeping an eye on the temperature, the children listened to records on their gramophone and ate the olive paste which was made for them to keep them occupied. When the pieces were removed from the furnace there were cries of joy and surprise, for the children never knew what had happened to the enamels and oxides, what would be added or separated or joined together. Back in the house, they unloaded their baskets full of dishes, plates and vases, spreading their masterpieces out on the table before their admiring parents.

Christmas Eve at Les Collettes

Opening the door that morning, Aline discovered a blanket of white frost surrounding the house. The grass shone and cracked like ice, and the entire hillside shivered. On this Christmas Eve, the Midi had disguised itself as Northern France. The preparations for the feast had begun the day before. Old Louise, accompanied by Baptistin, went early to the market, which overflowed with poultry, fish, game and exotic fruit that day. This

*A*lthough he was suffering severely from rheumatism that had deformed him and was no longer able to get around, Renoir maintained a remarkable sense of inner peace and courage. "I don't have a moment's rest," he said. "But I shouldn't complain: so many others my age can no longer work! At least I'm still able to paint."

Renoir painting in Cagnes.

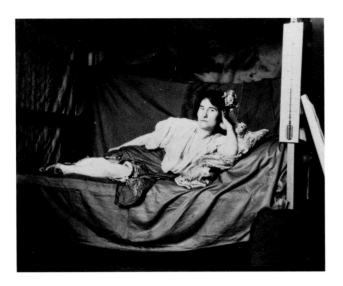

added flavor to the "Christmas Salad." Various shellfish were enjoyed, covered with a delicious sea urchin sauce. The plump turkey, stuffed with truffles, was laid on a bed of chestnuts. The dinner ended with a succession of thirteen desserts in the tradition of Provence and the South. Aline, being the epicurean that she was, could not resist the sweetness of the chocolate truffles, nor the unforgettable *orange crème* prepared by Old Louise. A large bowl of fruit sat on the buffet in the dining room among the bowls of dried fruits called "beggars," named after the color of the robes of monks from the Order of Beggars.

On the freshly starched white tablecloth, Aline set a delicate porcelain dinner service. The crystal glasses and the silverware's brilliance delightfully complemented the centerpiece composed of fresh flowers from the greenhouses.

The children chattered around the table, eager to open the presents piled under the tree. A good fire crackled in the fireplace. Renoir observed the scene with that mixture of irony and tenderness which was ever-present in his eyes. Comfortable in his chair, in the sweet warmth of the family, the old man smiled with ease.

was also the celebration of St Bartholomew of the Turkeys. The cook chose hers, plump, but not too fat. The week before, Madame Renoir, driven by Bistolfi, the new Italian driver, had gone to do her shopping in Nice. On the journey back, the Renault 14-20 CV was stuffed with packages of all sizes which were then stored in the boiler room. No one had been left out on this shopping spree; Aline had made a Christmas present list for the entire household.

With Coco's help, Gabrielle prepared the traditional nativity scene in a corner of the living room. Hills and dales were formed out of paper on which the wise men, led by the star, made their way to the manger where a tiny Jesus held out his little arms to them.

Pierre, who had arrived from Paris the evening before, lent his brothers a hand as they decorated the tree.

From early morning the kitchen resembled a beehive, with everyone helping out. Aline, while respecting tradition, drew up a menu in the spirit of the place: a marriage between the country and the nearby sea. To start with, there were a few delicately scrubbed and rinsed truffles, which

*B*ought by the city of Cagnes-sur-Mer in 1960, Les Collettes has become a museum. The glass studio (above) that Renoir built in the middle of an olive field no longer exists. In the other studio, located on the second floor of the house, it is as though nothing has changed since the painter's death in 1919. The wicker wheelchair in front of the easel, the palette, his paint box, paint brushes and tubes of paint are still where he last left them.

Left: Gabrielle in Renoir's studio in Cagnes, around 1910–1912.

Recipes

Menu designed by Renoir
for Madame Charpentier.
Private collection.

Soups

POTAGE CRÉCY
CRÉCY SOUP

In Renoir's day Parisian carrots from Meaux, Croissy and Crécy were highly thought of, especially the tiny bell carrots that Aline loved to prepare.

For 6 people

2lb small, tender carrots; 1 medium-sized onion; 8tbsp butter; salt and freshly ground pepper; sugar; 1½ quarts chicken stock (p. 187); ¾ cup round-grain rice; 6 sprigs of fresh chervil; 3 slices of stoneground bread; 2tbsp *crème fraîche* or heavy cream.

If the carrots are young, simply scrub them under running water and take off the tops. If the carrots are older, peel them with a vegetable peeler. Chop them finely, setting aside a few thin rounds. Peel and chop the onion. Melt half the butter in a stainless-steel saucepan. Before it turns brown, toss in the onion. Stir continuously for 5 minutes until the onion is soft. Add a pinch of salt and pepper, a pinch of sugar and the chopped carrots, reserving the thin rounds, which should be cooked separately for 20 minutes in a little of the stock.

Cover and cook over a low heat for 10 minutes, stirring occasionally. Heat up the stock and pour it over the carrots and onions. Cover the pan and simmer for approximately 6 to 8 minutes.

Add the rice, stir, and add several sprigs of fresh chervil, keeping aside a few sprigs to use for garnishing. Cover and cook for 15 to 20 minutes more.

When the rice is done (test by pressing a grain between finger and thumb; if it squashes easily, it is cooked), put the contents of the saucepan through a blender. Return the soup to the saucepan for reheating, taste, and adjust the seasoning if necessary.

Cut the bread slices into small sticks and fry in a pan with the remaining butter. Heat a soup tureen, pour the cream in the bottom, then pour in the soup, stir well and sprinkle the cooked carrot slices on the top. Garnish with chervil sprigs and serve immediately, accompanied by the crisp golden croûtons.

SOUPE À LA POUTINO
FISH PASTE SOUP

For 6 people

1lb of *poutino* (small fish roe and herbs paste); 2 leeks; 3 large tomatoes; 1 large onion; 3tbsp olive oil; 3 cloves of garlic; 1 fennel stem; 1 bouquet garni; pepper; 1 pinch saffron threads, steeped for 5 minutes in very hot water, or saffron powder; 8oz thick vermicelli.

This is a popular soup from Nice which dates back to Roman times.

Poutino (also known as *melet* or *pissalat*) is a paste obtained by mashing fish roe, traditionally from *blanchaille* (fish that is too small to be sold), with herbs and salt. This paste also provides the basis for another well-known dish originating from Nice called *pissaladière*.

First prepare the *poutino* by blending the roe from any small fish with the herbs. Peel, wash and dry the vegetables and slice them thinly. Sauté them in the olive oil over a gentle heat for 10 minutes, then, just before they begin to brown, add 1 quart of water. Peel and crush the garlic. Add the *poutino*, garlic, fennel, bouquet garni, pepper and the saffron powder (if saffron threads are being used these should be added towards the end, as indicated). Do not add any salt, as the *poutino* will already be salty enough.

Bring slowly to the boil and, once boiling, add the vermicelli. Let it simmer for 5 minutes (add saffron threads at this stage if being used instead of powder). Stir, remove from the heat, cover, and leave to steep for 5 minutes before serving with toasted croûtons brushed with garlic and sprinkled with some dried rosemary.

SOUPE AUX CHOUX D'ADRIENNE
ADRIENNE'S CABBAGE SOUP

Adrienne, who appeared in many of Renoir's paintings, was also quite adept in the kitchen. She was particularly fond of cooking the cabbage soups of the Achère region, especially during the icy winters. The use of bacon in this recipe gives the soup its distinctive taste.

For 6 people

6oz lightly-salted bacon; 2 medium-sized onions; 1 head of kale; 1 ½ quarts of light beef stock (p. 159); 2 large potatoes; 1 cured ham bone or pig's trotter; black pepper; mature cheese; stoneground bread, sliced.

Cut up the bacon, rinse, pat dry and dice. Place the bacon in a pot on a medium heat and let the pieces brown in their own fat.

Peel and finely chop the onions. Add them to the bacon, stir, lower the heat to a minimum and leave to cook.

Remove the stalk and outer leaves of the kale. Cut the heart into six pieces and chop the green leaves after washing them. Blanch for 2 minutes in boiling salted water, then strain.

Toss the chopped leaves into the pot. Do not stir. Heat up the stock. Peel the potatoes and cut them into chunks.

Stir the contents of the pot, add the ham bone or pig's trotter, pour in the stock and turn up the heat. When it begins to bubble, add the potatoes and the kale heart. Add a little pepper, cover, turn down the heat and leave to simmer gently for 25 minutes.

While the soup is simmering, crumble the cheese into a little bowl. Toast the bread in the oven. Place on the table together with the steaming soup, when ready. Once served, the soup can be garnished with toasted bread and ground pepper according to individual taste.

SOUPE À L'OIGNON
ONION SOUP

For 6 people

2tbsp butter; 2¹/₄lb onions; 1¹/₂ quarts light chicken or beef

stock; 1 bouquet garni with parsley stalks; salt and pepper; 1

pinch ground ginger; slices of toasted bread; 5oz grated

comté cheese (or nearest equivalent).

Peel and finely chop the onions. Melt the butter in a heavy-based casserole at low to medium heat. Throw the onions in the butter, spreading them out evenly, cover the casserole and let them sweat. When they are tender and translucent, stir them with a wooden spoon until they become golden and taste faintly of caramel.

Heat the stock with the bouquet garni. Pour onto the onions, stir, add salt, pepper and the ginger. When the liquid begins to bubble, turn the heat down to a minimum, cover almost completely and leave to simmer for 30 minutes. Taste and adjust the seasoning accordingly. Remove the bouquet garni and immediately serve the soup with a toasted, crusty baguette, coarsely ground pepper, and grated cheese.

This is the basic good old-fashioned version of onion soup (plain water was sometimes used instead of stock) which Renoir often enjoyed with his friends when they dined together at the local café.

This rather simple soup was subtly enriched for the late-night clientèle. To make this more extravagant version, remove the soup from the heat once it is ready and, using a whisk or fork, whip in two egg yolks, well separated from the whites, and a small glass of cognac or a slightly smaller glass of port.

Put the pieces of toast in the heated soup tureen, pour in the soup and top with some freshly grated cheese. Put until the broiler until the cheese melts, bubbles and turns coppery gold in color.

Appetizers and Side Dishes

OMELETTE AU LARD
POUR MONET ET POUR DEUX
BACON OMELET, FOR
MONET AND TWO OTHERS

This recipe is certainly much more palatable than the rancid bacon omelet that Renoir and Monet reluctantly ate one day in a small village near Barbizon, where they had gone in search of subjects for painting . . .

For 2 people

3¹/₂ oz thick-cut bacon; 1tsp fat or bacon drippings; 6 eggs; 1tbsp milk (heated and left to cool); salt and pepper; parsley or other herbs.

Remove the rind from the bacon and cut into small pieces.

Boil for 1 minute, drain and pat dry. Using a thin strip of cloth, rub drippings on to the bottom of a heavy-based frying pan. Place the pan over a medium heat, and when very hot throw in the bacon. Shake the pan from side to side over the heat until the meat is browned.

Beat together the eggs, milk, salt and pepper. Chop the parsley and set it aside.

Remove the bacon from the heat and place on paper towels to soak up excess fat.

Pour the fat out of the pan and scrape the bottom, but do not clean or wipe it. Return to the heat and toss in the remaining drippings. When the fat starts to sizzle, pour in all the egg mixture.

Let the mixture settle on the bottom of the pan and form a solid bed. Sprinkle the bacon on top. Tilt the pan with one hand while using a wooden spatula with the other to make sure all the uncooked egg runs under to touch the base of the pan so that all the egg mixture cooks evenly.

While the omelet is still slightly runny, with the consistency of scrambled eggs, sprinkle on some parsley (or any herb of your choice) and immediately turn off the heat.

Holding the pan firmly by the handle, lift and bang down to detach the omelet from the bottom. Then shake the pan to shift the omelet to one side. With one swift movement, flip one-third of the omelet so that it folds over onto itself. Do the same with the other side, so that you produce an omelet that is folded over like a wallet.

Slide on to a heated plate and serve immediately, with a green salad tossed in a sharp mustard vinaigrette.

ŒUFS BROUILLÉS AUX TRUFFES
SCRAMBLED EGGS WITH TRUFFLES

Madame Charpentier's Menu

The scrambled eggs served for dinner at the Charpentiers were accompanied by slices of toasted brioche.

For 6 people

1 large fresh truffle; 12 fresh eggs; 7tbsp butter;1¹/₃ cups extra thick *crème fraîche* or heavy cream; salt and freshly ground pepper.

Clean the truffle under a trickle of cold running water, using a soft nailbrush. Dry with a thin piece of cloth and place along with the unshelled eggs in a hermetically sealed jar. Leave at room temperature for 48 hours. It is important to make sure the atmosphere is neither too hot nor too cold.

When you are ready to prepare for the meal, open the jar and break the eggs one by one into a ramekin mold, and then slide them into a mixing bowl. Season, beat with a fork and set aside.

Place the truffle on to a flat plate and cut into 1 inch/2.5 cm thick rounds, then cut the rounds into thin strips.

Using softened butter, grease the base and sides of a frying pan. Prepare a double-boiler by filling a large saucepan, big enough to hold the frying pan, half-full of water and place over a medium heat. Quickly pour the eggs into the frying pan and rest it in the saucepan. Stir constantly with a wooden spatula, scraping the coagulated egg off the sides and bottom of the pan. Keep stirring until a creamy, homogeneous consistency is achieved. Remove from the heat and stir in the cream. When well blended, mix in the truffle strips. Season to taste and serve immediately in a heated porcelain bowl (never in anything silver-plated).

Instead of truffle, finely chopped herbs, ham, tomatoes, spinach or shellfish can be used.

FRITURE DE GUINGUETTE
FISH-FRY

This fried fish dish from the banks of the Seine and the Marne should be eaten hot and with the fingers, accompanied by a light, fruity, unpretentious table wine (preferably a vin de Suresnes *but any* vin de pays *will do).*

Cezanne's son Paul would net minnows in the rivers of Essoyes, and Marie Corot would fry them up in light oil.

For 6 people

4¹/₂lb small fish; salt; milk; flour; oil.

Don't try to complicate this simple dish, a longtime favorite of weekending Parisians. Any small freshwater fish will do: gudgeon, roach or, if nothing else is available, river or even sea smelts.

Rub the fish with a dry, stiff cloth. They are too small to be properly gutted and cleaned; a small squeeze with the thumb on the under-belly will force the bladder and intestines out through the hole in the abdomen, leaving the flesh intact.

Put the fish in a salted pan filled with some warm milk and leave them to soak for

about 20 minutes. Then drain and dry them
and roll them in flour. Pick them up three at a
time and shake off any excess flour.

Prepare a large pot of cooking oil, and
when it is hot (but not smoking) throw in the
fish a handful at a time. If they can be moved
freely in the oil and are not all bunched up
against one another they will fry quickly to a
golden crispness.

Repeat the procedure as often as is
necessary, and each time you remove the fish,
place them on kitchen towel to soak up the fat.
Then transfer them to a pan poised over a pot
of boiling water to keep warm. Serve with
parsley and lemon wedges.

ANCHOÏADE
ANCHOVY BUTTER

For 6 people

18 anchovy fillets in salt; ¹/₂ cup of cold milk; 1 large garlic clove; 1tbsp red wine vinegar; freshly ground pepper; 4tbsp olive oil.

Rinse the anchovy fillets under running water to remove as much of the salt as possible and any bones that may be left. Spread them out on a dish, cover with milk and leave to stand for approximately 1 hour in a cool place. Put to one side.

Meanwhile, peel and crush the garlic.

Drain, rinse and dry the anchovies and remove any remaining bones. Slice the fillets into small pieces and pulverize them into a smooth paste, using either a mortar and pestle or the back of a fork against the side of a bowl. Set aside.

Add the vinegar to the crushed garlic with a little black pepper and mix well. Gradually blend in the olive oil.

Mix the anchovy and garlic pastes together, kneading gently until a smooth and creamy paste is formed.

Toast some large slices of wholemeal bread and spread each slice with a generous helping of anchovy butter, forcing it well into the bread with the flat of a knife.

The people from Provence, who don't normally eat butter, call this unctuous sauce *anchoïade* and serve it frequently with raw vegetables, such as celery stalks, thin slices of raw red pepper, shelled yellow beans or small purple artichokes which they fondly call *mousso de cat* (cat's nose). They also use *anchoïade* to

baste grilled lamb, in meat stews such as *pot-au-feu*, or as an accompaniment to *poumo d'amour* (see the recipe for Cézanne's baked tomatoes, page 171).

JAMBON PERSILLÉ
HAM IN ASPIC

For 6 people

1 smoked shoulder of ham weighing 8–9lb; 2 blanched calves' trotters; 1 veal knuckle (optional); 1 bouquet garni (a celery stalk and the dark top leaves of a leek tied together with parsley stems); 1 large onion studded with 2 cloves; 4 medium-sized carrots; 1 bottle *aligoté* (crisp, fresh white burgundy); salt; 1tbsp coarsely ground pepper; 1 pinch allspice; 3 garlic cloves; 8 shallots; 1 bunch of parsley; 1 sprig of tarragon.

Rinse the salt from the ham by running water over it for 12 hours. Place the ham in a large cooking pot, cover with water and cook on a low heat. When the water begins to boil, turn down the heat to a minimum and leave to simmer for 25 minutes. If the trotters have not yet been blanched, put them in with the ham and remove them when the water first begins to simmer.

Drain the ham, rinse out the pot, half-fill it with water and put it back on the heat.

Remove the rind and bones from the ham. When the water in the pot is boiling, combine the ham with the trotters, bouquet garni, onion, carrots and wine (veal knuckle would make the flavor even more robust, but it is not essential). Make sure that there is enough water to cover all the ingredients. Let it simmer with the lid partially on until the ham is tender enough to mash with a spoon. This should take approximately 1¹/₂ hours. Add salt if necessary. Pepper and all-spice should be added later, about 30 minutes before the ham is cooked.

Remove the ham and trotters. Take a ladleful of the liquid and pour into a small bowl. Leave the rest of the liquid simmering over a low heat. The liquid in the bowl should solidify as it cools. When this occurs, remove the pot from the heat.

Cut the ham into chunks 1–2 inches/ 2.5–5 cm thick or shred it coarsely.

Finely chop the garlic, shallots, parsley and tarragon. Before taking out the meat, place a large earthenware baking dish in the refrigerator. The classic *bourguignon* terrine, which is a large, white bowl with a bell-shaped rim, is recommended for this recipe. Strain the cooking juices which had been set aside to cool through a layer of very cold and damp cheesecloth to remove the fat. Then coat the sides of the dish with the liquid to form a layer of jelly. Take the remaining cooking juices and strain, using the cheesecloth to remove the fat. Arrange a bed of ham and trotters on the bottom of the dish, followed by a layer of chopped herbs, garlic and shallots. Continue to alternate the two, ending with a layer of meat.

Pour in all the cooking juices. Allow to cool at room temperature before covering with plastic wrap and refrigerating. Slip the ham aspic out of its mold and serve in thick slices. If you are taking it to a picnic, as Renoir liked to do, leave it in the terrine and serve with gherkins and onions.

HURE DE SANGLIER DU PERE RENARD

PERE RENARD'S POTTED BOAR'S HEAD

Gabrielle Renard's father was a keen hunter, and during winter at Essoyes the Renoirs and the Renards often ate wild boar. Jean reminisced about how they would all argue over who should get the most coveted piece—the head. This recipe ensured that peace was maintained as it provided plenty of everything for everyone.

For 6 people

¹/₂lb boar's meat; large piece of pork rind; ³/₄lb bacon; coarse or sea salt; crushed black and white peppercorns; 2 small glasses brandy or Champagne marc; 1 boar's head (scalded, cleaned and boned by a butcher) with bones; 1tsp allspice; 3 sprigs of dried thyme; 3 sage leaves; 3 bay leaves; 1 bottle dry white wine; 1 bunch of parsley; 1 egg; 1¹/₂ cups pistachios; 2 carrots; 1 large onion studded with 2 cloves; 1 celery stalk; 1¹/₂ quarts beef stock.

The night before the meal, carefully remove all the veins and stringy parts from the boar meat.

Trim the fat from the pork rind and set aside for later. Cut the boar's meat and bacon into small pieces and grind in a meat grinder or food mill. Combine with salt, pepper and a glass of brandy or marc. Cover with plastic wrap and refrigerate. Flambé the head and bones with the remaining brandy or marc.

Place the head in a large bowl and sprinkle with pepper, allspice, crushed thyme leaves, chopped sage and bay leaves. Pour in two glasses of white wine and marinate, covered, for 12 hours in the refrigerator. On the day of the meal, drain the head and stuff with the chopped meat, to which you have added chopped parsley, beaten egg, pistachios, salt, pepper and the herbs left over from the marinade. Truss the stuffed head as you would a roast (you can also sew it into cheesecloth).

Line the bottom of a large pot with the pork rind, fat side facing down. Cover with thick slices of peeled carrots and onions, the celery stalk wrapped in parsley and the stripped sprigs of thyme. Arrange the boar's head in the pot surrounded by the other ingredients. Add the bones and the pork rind fat.

Cover everything with beef stock and the remaining white wine, the marinade juice and top up with more stock if need be to fill the pot almost to the brim. Cover and bring slowly to a boil. Reduce to a simmer and skim regularly for 5 hours. Allow to cool before removing the boar's head. Remove the trussing string or cheesecloth and place the head in a terrine slightly larger than itself. Ladle the broth on top. Serve chilled, cut into slices.

BOUQUET GARNI

A bouquet garni is frequently used in French cooking to add flavor to soups, stews, stock and other savory dishes. It is usually made up of a bay leaf, a sprig of thyme, and two or three sprigs of parsley with their stalks. If the herbs are fresh you can simply tie them together with a thread so they can be easily lifted out of the dish when it is ready. If they are dried, tie them up in a small piece of cheesecloth. You can also add a clove of garlic and, for an authentic taste of Provence, a piece of dried orange rind.

SALADE FRANCILLON OU JAPONAISE

FRANCILLON OR JAPANESE SALAD

At the time this recipe was first created, around 1887, Alexandre Dumas Fils, the author of Francillon, *recommended through one of his characters, the maid Annette, that* Château-Yquem *be used for the marinade.*

For 6 people

1¹/₂ lb small potatoes; chicken stock; ³/₄ lb Jerusalem artichokes; sea salt and pepper; strong mustard; white wine vinegar; extra-virgin olive oil; 1 bunch of chives; 2 cups Chablis; 24 mussels; 3 hard-boiled eggs; 1 truffle.

Cook the small potatoes in the chicken stock and the artichokes in salted boiling water.

Prepare the savory vinaigrette sauce by combining the sea salt and a spoonful of mustard in the white wine vinegar. Emulsify with a small amount of olive oil before tossing in some chopped herbs and adding pepper.

When the potatoes are cooked, drain them and cover to keep them warm. One by one peel each potato while hot and slice into a bowl of Chablis. Immediately transfer with a slotted spoon to the vinaigrette sauce. Stir. Mix the potatoes delicately with the cooked and drained artichokes.

Prepare the mussels by following the Berneval recipe (see p.150) with the exception that they should be cooked in Chablis and the shells removed. Slice the hard-boiled eggs and mix with the mussels.

Serve in a salad bowl and decorate with truffle slices.

RISSOLES À LA CHEVREUSE
CHEVREUSE RISSOLES

Rissoles *were the epitome of gastronomy at the turn of the century in France, and were served on special occasions. They were prepared using cock's brain, crest and kidney together with truffles. It was the truffles and the* bouchées à la reine *(vol-au-vents) that made Murer, the poet and pastry-maker, friend and patron of the Impressionists, a celebrity.*

For 6 people

2 sweetbreads, blanched and cleaned; wine vinegar; 1³/₄ cups poultry or veal stock (see recipes p. 187); 4 shallots; 2¹/₂ oz button mushrooms; 3tbsp butter; salt and pepper; 1 cup béchamel sauce (see recipe p. 188); 1 pinch of ground nutmeg; 3tbsp thick *crème fraîche* or heavy cream; 1 bouquet garni made with parsley and chervil; 1lb 6oz puff pastry; flour; 1 egg (optional).

Ask the butcher to clean and blanch the sweetbreads. Otherwise soak the uncleaned sweetbreads in cold water, to which a spoonful of vinegar was added, for an hour. Then blanch for 5 minutes as the water is brought to a simmer. Remove them from the hot water and put them under running cold water. Make sure all the fat and nerves have been removed and cook them for 10 minutes in the simmering stock. Then turn off the heat and let them poach. Remove them and pat dry using paper towels.

The sweetbreads will later on be cut into 18 small portions.

Prepare the sauce that will be used to coat the sweetbreads. Finely chop the peeled shallots. Cut off the gritty ends of the mushrooms and clean them under running water (do not soak them), then chop the stalks into thin rounds and finely dice the tops.

Melt the butter in a stainless steel saucepan over a medium heat. Add the shallots and cook them for 5 minutes until they soften. Then add the mushroom stalks, stir, and 2 minutes later add in the diced mushrooms. Season with salt and pepper and cover three-quarters of the saucepan. Let them give out moisture for 5 minutes then add the béchamel sauce, mixing it in carefully with the ground nutmeg, and finally the cream. Stir the mixture continuously.

Finely chop the parsley and chervil and set aside on a plate.

Lay the puff pastry flat, in a rectangle 1 inch thick, and then cut out circles 4–5inches in diameter. Allow the puff pastry to rest. In the meantime sprinkle flour over the sweetbreads, dip them in the béchamel base mix, and then into the chopped herbs.

Rest each portion of sweetbread on half a circle of puff pastry. Using a palette knife, wet the edges of the pastry circles, over ¹/₂ inch or so, and fold up the circles into half moons. Press hard, or better still pinch the two layers together to seal tightly.

Whisk an egg. (If only an egg yolk is available mix it with one spoonful of milk which has been heated then cooled.) Using a brush, coat the rissoles with the egg just before cooking them.

The rissoles can be set aside, wrapped up in a cloth (before coating them with egg), in a cool area until fried or baked.

Heat up a big pan full of oil and dip in the rissoles, six or eight at a time—no more, in order that they may be stirred around easily to brown them.

Alternatively, preheat the oven to 425°F and place the rissoles in a baking dish on the the middle shelf. After 6 minutes, lower the temperature to 350°F. Cook for a further 6 to 8 minutes and then serve.

Fish

BUISSON D'ÉCREVISSES
CRAYFISH PLATTER

For 6 people

5lb live freshwater crayfish (approximately 50); 3³/₄
quarts/7¹/₂ pints fish stock (see recipe p. 186); 1 pimento; 1
clove.

Sauce

1 quart fish stock; 10tbsp softened butter; 4 sprigs fresh
chervil, stripped; 4 parsley sprigs; 2 pinches cayenne pepper;
1tsp white and black pepper.

Do not try to shell the crayfish; this will
only damage the flesh, without in any way
improving their flavor. Soak them for 48 hours
in fresh water, or for 3 hours in a large
container of cold milk.

The fish stock can be prepared in advance
and kept in the refrigerator until just before
use. Add the pimento and clove and place over
a medium heat.

While the fish stock is reheating, remove
the crayfish from the water or milk and
rinse them thoroughly. The fish stock should
be brought to a full boil over a heat which,
when cooking begins, can be raised still higher
so that it can be reheated quickly.

Plunge the crayfish into the boiling stock
all at once, cover and turn the heat up higher.
Allow the crayfish to cook initially for 2 minutes
with the cover on, then, depending on their
size, another 1 or 2 minutes uncovered and
gently stirred. Drain and set aside in a covered
dish while you prepare the sauce.

Pour approximately 1 quart of stock
through a colander into a saucepan. Place over a
brisk heat and reduce by half.

Cut the butter into small pieces. Remove
the leaves from the chervil sprigs and finely
chop the parsley.

When the liquid has reduced, lower the
heat and briskly whisk in the butter piece by
piece. Whisk in the cayenne and black and
white pepper with the last piece, remove from
the heat and gently whisk in the herbs.

Warm two gravy dishes in boiling water
and fill them both with sauce.

Serve immediately with a good dry white
wine and a basket of warm toast wrapped in a
napkin. The recipe can also be used for shrimp
or scampi.

In Renoir's day, in the homes of the rich French
bourgeoisie, crayfish were usually served cold on a
multi-tiered platter, decorated with parsley and
accompanied by a choice of sauces.

L'OURSINADO D'ALINE
ALINE'S SEA URCHIN SAUCE

For 6 people

1 cup béchamel sauce (see recipe p. 188); 12 sea urchins;

1 egg yolk; salt and freshly ground pepper.

First prepare the béchamel sauce and keep it warm in a double boiler.

Open the sea urchins, using sharp pointed scissors. Begin cutting by inserting the scissor blade into the hole and carefully cut in two, then scoop out the orange parts with a teaspoon. Place the flesh in a colander and press with the back of a wooden spoon to extract all the flesh from the membrane. Pour a little strained sea urchin water over the membranes, press again and scrape the inside walls of the sea urchins with a knife to obtain as much flesh as possible.

Add the egg yolk into the béchamel. Whisk thoroughly, then add the sea urchins and mix with a spoon until smooth.

In the South of France, this sauce is served with fish broiled or poached in fish stock, poached cod, or simply poured over garlic and thyme croûtons (see also the recipe for Porgy Provençal, right).

For a lighter version of this sauce, without béchamel, beat together two egg yolks, a glass of strained sea urchin water and $^1/_2$ cup of olive oil in a small, stainless steel pot. Stir these ingredients together in a double boiler until the mixture thickens. Add in the puréed sea urchins, mix well and season to taste, using liberal amounts of coarsely ground pepper.

DAURADE À LA PROVENÇALE
PORGY PROVENÇAL

For 6 people

1 porgy (approximately 3lb); 4 medium onions; 1 medium carrot; 1 leek; 1 fenugreek with its "tuft"; 2 garlic cloves; 2 flat parsley sprigs, savory, dill; 2 unwaxed lemons; $^1/_2$ cup dry white wine; 1 cup fish stock (see recipe p. 186); salt and pepper; 3tbsp olive oil; 1 cup sea urchin sauce (see recipe left).

Scale the fish without damaging the flesh. Remove the fins, gut, wash and dry. Keep in a cool place. Peel the vegetables, wash and cut them into thin slices. Be sure to keep the green fenugreek "tuft". Peel and crush the garlic, remove the leaves from the stems of the herbs and set aside. Tie the stems together. Wash and dry the lemons and slice into rounds.

Take a rectangular or oval flameproof oven dish, large enough to hold the fish. In the bottom, lay the vegetable slices, the garlic and the bouquet garni. Add some white wine, stock, salt and pepper and put over a medium heat. Bring to the boil and, when bubbling, reduce the heat to minimum and simmer for 5 minutes, then turn off the heat. Leave to cool. Preheat the oven to 425°F. Finely chop the herbs and fenugreek.

Salt and pepper the interior of the fish and slide the chopped herbs and about three lemon slices inside. Close the fish tightly and place it in the dish. Douse well with the remaining stock, cover with the lemon slices, pour over some oil and place in the oven for 15 to 20 minutes. Baste from time to time with the cooking juices.

MOULES COMME À BERNEVAL
MUSSELS BERNEVAL

For 6 people

4 quarts Dieppe mussels, if available; 3 shallots; 1 medium-sized onion; 5tbsp butter; 1 bouquet garni (fresh thyme, bay leaf, parsley stems, celery stalk: optional); 1 tomato; 1 slice of lemon rind; 2 glasses white wine; 1tbsp light cream; 3 parsley sprigs; salt and pepper.

Scrub and clean the mussels, then drain.

Peel the shallots and onion and chop them finely. Melt the butter in a large pot (with a tight-fitting lid and handles). Sauté the shallots and onions.

Prepare the bouquet garni with the thyme, bay leaf and parsley stalks, keeping the leaves to one side. In Normandy, a small stick of celery is often added to this dish and can be added here if so desired.

Wash the tomato and remove the stem. Squeeze gently to remove the watery seeds and chop up.

When the shallots and onions are tender, add the tomato, bouquet garni, celery, lemon rind, pepper, and wine. When the liquid begins to boil drop in the mussels. Turn up the heat. As soon as they start to open, cover and secure the lid by tying a damp twisted dish cloth over it and through both handles. Shake the pot vigorously and place back on the heat, uncovered. Remove the opened mussels, still in their shells. Remove one shell from each and place in a large serving dish. Cover the dish and keep warm.

When all of the mussels have been transferred to the serving dish, filter the stock into a small pot and add a tablespoonful of single cream and the chopped parsley leaves. Whisk over a brisk heat, add salt and pepper and pour over the mussels. Serve in preheated shallow soup bowls.

You will find another use for mussels — which Renoir painted women fishing for during his stay in Normandy — in the *Salade Francillon* recipe (see p. 144).

BAR POCHÉ AUX ÉCREVISSES
POACHED SEA BASS
WITH CRAYFISH

For 6 people

1 bass (weighing approximately 2^3/$_4$lb; 1 bouquet garni; salt and pepper; 2 quarts *fumet* (see recipe p. 186).

Gut and clean the bass but do not remove the scales or the fins. Cut off two-thirds of the tail. Fill the belly with the roe if there was any, the bouquet garni and seasoning. Close and wrap the fish in parchment paper and tie it up. Place on the grid of a fish kettle and pour cold strained *fumet* over it. Cover and place over medium heat until the *fumet* starts to quiver. Lower the heat to a minimum but keep it slightly simmering. Poach the bass (8 to 10 minutes for 1 inch thickness). Turn off the heat and allow it to cook through for another 3 minutes.

Check that it is cooked enough by poking a skewer into the gills. The skewer should go through the flesh easily.

Lift out the grid and let the bass slide off it into a preheated fish dish. Cut the ties, remove the parchment paper and immediately

remove the skin and gills using a small knife. Surround the fish with hot crayfish tails and serve with any of the following sauces: lemon butter, white butter sauce, herb butter, Hollandaise or Nantua sauce (see recipe p. 188).

If no fish kettle is available, use an oval casserole big enough to hold the fish and improvise a grid with aluminum foil doubled up, slightly raised along the edges and twisted at both ends so that you can handle the fish comfortably.

BOUILLABAISSE D'ALINE
ALINE'S BOUILLABAISSE

For 6 people

4¹/₂ lb fish (for an authentic *bouillabaisse*, at least 4 different varieties of fish should be used: scorpion or hog fish is essential, monkfish, red gurnard, wrasse, and John Dory are traditional choices; striped bass, cod, red snapper, hake, sole, flounder, squid and eel are also appropriate); 1¹/₂ tbsp olive oil; 1lb large potatoes, peeled and thinly sliced; ¹/₂ tsp saffron threads; *rouille* (see recipe p. 187); 12 to 16 thin slices of stale or sun-dried bread.

Stock

2 leeks, cleaned and sliced; 1 large onion, peeled and chopped; 2 garlic cloves, peeled and crushed; 2 dry fennel twigs; 4 tomatoes, quartered; 1 thyme twig; ¹/₂ bay leaf; 3inches orange rind (dried in the oven) 2¹/₄ lb rock fish, or nearest equivalent with fish bones, heads and trimmings; salt and pepper.

Marinade

2tbsp olive oil; ¹/₂ tsp saffron powder; 1 parsley sprig and stalk; dried savory, oregano, and marjoram; 1¹/₂ tbsp Pernod.

Clean and trim the fish; leave the smaller ones whole and cut the larger ones into chunks or thick slices. Keep the tails, heads and trimmings for the stock.

In a large, shallow bowl make the marinade with the olive oil, herbs, half a teaspoon of saffron powder and half the Pernod. Rub the fish pieces inside and out with the marinade until they take on a saffron-yellow color. Leave them in the marinade for an hour while preparing the stock, turning them over from time to time with a wooden spatula.

Prepare the stock. In a large pot, place the tender green parts of the leeks (setting the white parts aside for later), chopped onion, crushed garlic, fennel, quartered tomatoes, thyme, bay leaf, orange rind, the rock fish and the fish bones, heads and trimmings. Sprinkle with olive oil and cook over a low heat, stirring occasionally.

After 15 minutes, pour in 3¹/₂ quarts water (cooks from Provence also add a large glass of white Var wine at this point), salt (but do not add pepper yet), and boil rapidly for 30 minutes.

Pour the contents of the pot through a food mill or thick strainer placed over a large mixing bowl. Press with a big spoon to extract as much juice as possible. Season with salt and pepper and set aside.

In a large pot heat heat 1¹/₂ tablespoons of olive oil. Toss in the white part of the leeks, after having washed, dried and sliced them, together with the potatoes, cut into ¹/₈ inch slices. Pour in the stock and the rest of the Pernod. Bring to a slow boil over medium heat, then count to ten before raising the temperature and boiling rapidly.

Add the saffron threads and then the fish, according to their size and firmness. Start with the eel, squid, monkfish, wrasse and the like; after 5 minutes add scorpion fish and the John

Dory; and 5 minutes later all the delicate or small fish, such as sole, flounder, red snapper or gurnards. Add the marinade, lower the heat and cook for another 2 to 3 minutes.

Fill a large soup tureen with stock and a shallow dish with fish and potatoes. Put small bowls of rouille on the table, along with plates of dried bread rubbed with garlic. Serve in hot soup plates with a well-chilled white wine from Provence.

MERLANS À LA BERCY
BERCY WHITING

Parisian bistros often poached this delicately fleshed fish in wines from the Quai de Bercy, the great wine warehouse district of Paris. A more popular preparation, however, was to poach it in milk or beer, then fry it to a golden brown and arrange it "en colère", with the tail "angrily" wedged into the mouth. These were served on embossed paper, with fried parsley and mustard.

Camille, who ran the kitchen of Renoir's favorite neighborhood restaurant, prepared whiting in both of these styles, and also used the sauce described here for liver and kidneys.

For 6 people

6 whiting or hake, 9oz each; 2 parsley sprigs; 3 shallots; 8tbsp butter; salt and pepper; 1³/₄ cups dry white wine; 1 lemon.

Gut the fish. Wash and dry them with a paper towels, removing the remaining fine scales which are still attached to the skin.

Finely chop the parsley stalks and shallots. Mix them with an equal amount of butter. Season with salt and pepper and place a small amount inside each fish. If there is any roe inside, do not remove.

Make a bed of chopped shallots and parsley in a well-buttered baking dish and arrange the fish on top, head to tail. If any shallots and parsley remain, use them to cover the fish. Salt and pepper to taste.

Preheat the oven to 475°F. Pour the white wine around but not on top of the fish. Cut the remaining butter into small pieces and dot over the fish. Place over a brisk heat. When the wine begins to bubble furiously, transfer to the oven for 10 minutes. Baste the fish 2 or 3 times with its juice while cooking.

Halve the lemon, then cut each half into three pieces—one for each fish. Heat the serving plates.

Serve the fish with steamed potatoes or Vollard's creole rice, moistened with fish stock (see recipes p. 176 and p. 186) on top.

HARENGS À LA JOSÉPHINE
JOSEPHINE'S HERRINGS

Madame Renoir ordered her fish from her neighbor Josephine, who lived next to the Château des Brouillards. Josephine would walk the streets of the Montmartre district hawking her fish, but Madame would only buy if they were offered at a very good price—proof for her that the fish were fresh and caught locally. Herring was always a bargain, and these she would grill over charcoal and serve with a mustard sauce.

For 6 people

6 fresh herrings, preferably containing roe; juice of ¹/₂ lemon; 3tbsp flour; 2 medium-sized eggs; ¹/₂ cup butter; 3tbsp groundnut oil; 1 heaped tbsp coarse ground mustard; salt and pepper.

Sauce

5oz/125g butter; lemon juice.

Dry the herrings with a kitchen towel and set aside their roe.

Place them in a deep dish and sprinkle with the juice of half a lemon. Set aside.

Cover a large plate with flour. Crack the eggs into a bowl and beat lightly with a fork. Add a dash of mustard, season with salt and pepper and continue beating. Pour into a shallow dish.

Melt the butter in a saucepan, adding salt and pepper. Add the rest of the mustard and mix with a wooden spoon. Thin with a little lemon juice and set aside in a warm place.

Drain and dry the herrings. Dip them, one by one, first into the egg mixture and then in the flour.

Heat a small amount of butter and oil in a large non-stick frying pan. Add the fish and fry for 3 minutes, until lightly browned. Turn over and fry for another minute.

Remove the fish with a slotted spoon and place on a kitchen towel. Cover them in warm sauce and serve immediately with toasted bread, accompanied by steamed potatoes or potato salad.

BRANDADE DE MORUE
CREAMED SALT COD

For 6 people

1¼ lb salt cod fillets; 2 garlic cloves; 1½ cups olive oil; 1¼ cups whole milk, heated then chilled, or light cream; salt and freshly ground pepper; 1 pinch of grated nutmeg.

Begin preparing the salt cod a day ahead. Rinse by leaving it under running water or soak it in water that is changed very frequently. Put a piece of wood or a plate on the bottom of the basin to collect the salt. This process should take at least 12 hours.

Drain the cod, cut it into several uniform pieces and put them into a large pot. Cover the cod completely with water and slowly bring to a simmer, being careful not to allow it to reach a boil.

Turn the heat down to a minimum and skim the foam off until the liquid is clear. Turn off the heat. Cover and leave to poach for 10 to 12 minutes.

Peel and crush the garlic.

Pour the oil into a small stainless steel saucepan (reserve 2 or 3 spoonfuls, which should be poured into a very large enamel or stainless steel pot). Pour the milk into another saucepan of the same size.

Drain the fish and remove the skin (though some chefs like to keep the particularly gelatinous parts of the white skin, which give a soft, thick texture to the flesh) and then remove the bones.

Break the cod into flakes and drop it into the large pot. Heat the two small saucepans over a low heat, and the large one over a medium heat.

Add the garlic to the cod flakes and beat the mixture into a paste with a wooden spoon. Pour in two spoonfuls of hot oil. Mix this thoroughly together before adding two spoonfuls of hot milk.

Repeat this process, mixing in oil and milk until until the contents of the pot take on the smooth, white and airy consistency of puréed potatoes. Add pepper and nutmeg to taste. The cod will also benefit from a pinch of sea salt.

If the *brandade* must wait a while before being served, cover the surface with a layer of the scalded and reheated milk and a dollop of light cream. This will prevent it from drying out. Keep warm in a covered double boiler.

Serve the *brandade* with toasted country-style bread or garlic croûtons pan-fried in olive oil. Gourmets like to serve it in a silver timbale crowned with flowers.

Meat, Poultry and Game

LAPIN À L'AIL ET AUX OLIVES
RABBIT WITH GARLIC AND OLIVES

For 6 people

1 rabbit (approximately 4 to 5lbs) with liver and heart; 1 large, fresh bay leaf; 2tbsp olive oil; 2tbsp red wine vinegar; 1 large thyme sprig; salt and black pepper; 5 garlic cloves; 1 small bunch of flat-leaf parsley; 3tbsp stoned black olives.

Cut the rabbit into six pieces: two thighs, two legs and two sides of ribs. Keep the neck and heart, which will make the sauce richer. The delicate liver should be cooked separately.

Crumble the bay leaf into a saucer. Choose a pot large enough to fit the rabbit pieces side by side. Heat the olive oil over a medium heat and when it "sings" add the rabbit pieces and fry until golden brown on both sides. Towards the end, add the whole liver and the coarsely chopped heart.

Pour the vinegar into a stainless steel saucepan and heat gently.

When the rabbit pieces are well done, scatter the thyme on top by rubbing the stems between the palms of your hands if it is dry, or by separating the leaves from the stems if the thyme is fresh. Add the bay leaf, salt and pepper and lower the heat.

Pour the warm vinegar over the rabbit pieces and cover carefully. Simmer slowly for 30 minutes.

Peel and crush the garlic. Remove the parsley leaves and chop finely. Check that all the olives are pitted and prepare the water for cooking the accompanying pasta — tagliatelle is recommended.

After 30 minutes, remove the neck and sprinkle the rabbit with the chopped parsley and garlic and olives. Stir with a wooden spoon and leave for a further 10 minutes over a low heat, uncovered.

Serve immediately in a large, preheated dish on a bed of tagliatelle or macaroni and cover with the sauce and olives.

NAVARIN DE MOUTON DE LA GRAND-LOUISE

OLD LOUISE'S MUTTON STEW

Like Madame Renoir, Old Louise was born in Essoyes. She cooked and occasionally posed for the artist. The hallways of the apartment on the Boulevard de Rochechouart were often filled with the tantalizing aroma of this stew.

For 6 people

1tbsp suet or groundnut oil; 2¹/₄ shoulder of mutton, cut into large cubes with bones; 1¹/₄ lb lamb breast, cut into chunks; 3 large onions; 2 medium-sized shallots; 1 large clove of garlic; 1 level tbsp flour; 1 large bouquet garni with parsley stems and small celery stalk; 1²/₃ cups chicken stock; 1 cup sparkling apple cider; 3 carrots; freshly ground pepper; 3 turnips; 3 large potatoes; salt.

Choose a pot large enough to allow the meat to be cooked without having to be piled up. Put it over a low heat and add the suet, so that it melts without browning.

Put in the mutton and lamb pieces. Sauté on one side until brown and then turn over, using a wooden spoon so as not to pierce the meat.

Meanwhile peel and quarter the onions and shallots. Peel the garlic and crush using the flat of a knife. Sift the flour and set aside.

Mix in the onion quarters. Prepare the bouquet garni: one fresh bay leaf, two sprigs of thyme, one of flat-leaf parsley, one leafy celery stalk, one clove wrapped in dark green leek leaves. Tie together with kitchen string.

Heat the stock until simmering. Turn off the heat.

Sprinkle flour on to the contents of the pot and stir well. Turn up the heat a little so that the flour cooks completely. When the flour has dissolved, pour the cider in and add the garlic and the bouquet garni. Grate a carrot into the pot. When the cider begins to bubble, pour in any remaining stock, add pepper and cover. Turn down the heat and simmer for 40 minutes.

Peel and cut the turnips into thick slices if they are long or into quarters if they are round. Do the same with the remaining carrots. Put them into the pot after 40 minutes and put the lid back on. Check the amount of liquid in the pot; if it is too low, add ¹/₂ cup of hot stock, or very hot water if none is available. Cover the pot again.

Peel and quarter the potatoes and soak them in fresh water. After the stew has cooked for an hour, add the potatoes to the other ingredients. Season with salt and pepper and continue cooking the stew for another 20 minutes with the lid on over a low heat until the meat is tender.

Warm a large platter. Take out the meat with a skewer and place it in the middle of the platter, bordered with vegetables. Remove the bouquet garni and the bones and pour the hot sauce over the meats.

Serve immediately with a very good dry cider and large, thick pieces of toasted bread for soaking up the sauce.

POT-AU-FEU DES COLLETTES
LES COLLETTES STYLE
BEEF STEW

Aline's mother's pot-au-feu *recipe was a regular feature of family dinners at Essoyes and Château des Brouillards.*

At Collettes, Aline adapted her mother's recipe, which called for a shoulder of mutton, by also adding a clove of garlic, two tomatoes, a slice of dried melon skin, and, just at the end, some dried tarragon.

She served the dish with strongly flavored herbs, a plateful of arugula or watercress, and a bowl of black olives.

For 6 people

1lb side of beef; 1lb beef knuckle; 2 marrow bones; 1 onion, studded with 2 cloves; 10 carrots; 3 turnips; 1 celery root; 5 leeks; 2 celery stalks; 2 parsley sprigs; 3 fresh thyme twigs; 3 bay leaves; 1 garlic clove; 14oz lean bacon; 1lb 6oz mutton shoulder; 1 veal knuckle, chopped in two; 2lb silverside; 5 juniper berries; sea salt, black and white pepper.

Put the side of beef, beef knuckle, 2 marrow bones (both wrapped in a piece of cheesecloth) and onion in a large pot. Cover with 5 quarts of cold water, place the pot over a high heat and bring to the boil. Skim until the liquid is clear, then lower the heat to a minimum and cook, uncovered, for approximately 2 hours.

Prepare the vegetables. Keep the dark green leek leaves and tie them up with the parsley stems, thyme and bay leaves to make a bouquet garni. Remove the marrow bones, keeping them in their cheesecloth bag. Add the bouquet garni, garlic and vegetables, as well as the bacon, mutton shoulder, veal knuckle, silverside, and a cheesecloth bouquet of juniper berries and pepper. Bring to the boil, skim completely and cook for 3 hours.

Turn off the heat and put the marrow bones back into the stock. Drain and transfer the meats and marrow bones (with their cheesecloth bags removed) on to a serving dish and surround with the cooked vegetables. Discard the onion, bouquet garni and herbs from the stock. Strain over a soup tureen and serve immediately, with slices of toasted bread, steamed or boiled potatoes, gherkins, sea salt and various coarse and smooth mustards.

FOIE DE VEAU BOURGEOISE
VEAL LIVERS BOURGEOISE

For 6 people

5oz pork fat; $^1/_2$ cup cognac; pepper; 1 fresh thyme twig;
2$^1/_4$lb veal liver; salt; 1 pig caul, rinsed; groundnut oil; butter;
6oz smoked pork belly or streaky bacon, chopped into small
pieces; 12 little carrots; 6 small onions; $^1/_2$ bottle white
burgundy, at room temperature; 1 bouquet garni.

Slice the pork fat into little strips and soak them in cognac, pepper and stripped thyme leaves. Cover with plastic wrap and leave for an hour at room temperature.

Drain the fat, and set aside the liquid for the sauce. Pierce the liver with a fork, remove the outer membrane, and season with salt and pepper. Place the liver on the caul and allow to dry. Sprinkle thyme over the entire surface of the liver and wrap the caul around it to make a package. Truss it up in the same manner as you would a roast.

Heat the groundnut oil and a knob of butter in a pot. Lightly brown the wrapped liver on both sides. Remove from the heat and keep warm.

Dice the strips of pork belly or bacon fat. Peel and chop the carrots and the onions. In the same pot, gently fry the bacon pieces, carrots and onions for 5 minutes, until golden brown. Push them to the sides of the pot to make room for the liver. Add any juice which has escaped from the liver, the wine, which should be at room temperature, bouquet garni and cognac marinade. Preheat the oven to 425°F.

As soon as the wine mixture begins to bubble transfer the pot to the oven. After 7 or 8 minutes lower the temperature to 400°F and bake for 1 hour.

Turn off the oven and leave its door ajar for another 5 minutes. Heat a serving platter, unwrap the liver, and arrange it on the platter, surrounded by the vegetables and bacon. Return the pot to the oven, still off, with the door open. Remove the bouquet garni and strain the sauce through a moistened piece of filter paper to get rid of excess fat.

Serve immediately, accompanied by a good white burgundy.

POULET RENOIR
CHICKEN RENOIR

For 6 people

1 free-range chicken (approximately 3$^1/_2$ lb) with giblets;
$^1/_2$ cup cognac; 1tbsp olive oil; 2 medium-sized onions;
2 medium tomatoes; 2 large cloves of garlic; 1 bouquet garni
(parsley, 1 sprig of bay leaves and 1 sprig of thyme); 1 knob
of butter; sea salt and black peppercorns; 4oz mushrooms;
4oz black olives.

Cut the chicken in pieces, clean the heart, the gizzard and remove any greenish parts of the liver (your butcher can do this for you). Leave the liver to soften in the cognac while the chicken is simmering.

Pour the oil into a heavy-based pot large enough to hold the chicken pieces easily. Place on a medium heat and gently fry the chicken pieces, wings, gizzard and the heart.

Peel and finely chop the onions. Skin the tomatoes and remove the seeds. Peel and crush one of the garlic cloves. Set aside some parsley

and the remaining garlic clove to make *persillade* (a mix of crushed garlic with parsley).

As each piece of chicken becomes golden, remove it to a warm covered dish. Discard the cooking oil and, without cleaning the pot, melt the butter in it.

Add the chopped onion and stir for 4 minutes until tender. Add the tomatoes, crushed garlic, chicken, the parsley stems tied together with the thyme and bay leaves, some sea salt and crushed black peppercorns. Moisten with a cup of warm water. Cover. Turn the heat down and leave to simmer for 20 minutes over a very low heat while stirring from time to time.

Clean the mushrooms (these should preferably be wild, but if not available, button

mushrooms will do). Add them to the sauce and cover immediately.

Throw the drained black olives (stoned olives give a stronger, better taste) into the pot and add the liver. Cover and wait 5 to 7 minutes before pouring on the cognac. Uncover and leave for 3 minutes, until the cognac has evaporated and only its aroma remains.

Remove the bouquet garni and pour everything into a deep serving dish. Sprinkle with *persillade* and serve immediately with rice or thick macaroni.

COTES DE PORC
SAUCE CHARCUTIERE
PORK CHOPS
WITH CHARCUTIERE SAUCE

For 6 people

6 prime pork chops (300g each);1 pinch grated nutmeg; salt and pepper; ¹/₂tsp oil or suet.

Sauce

12 scallions or pearl onions; 1¹/₂tbsp butter; 1¹/₂tbsp dry white wine or sparkling apple cider; ¹/₃ cup beef stock; 1 cup small gherkins; 2 heaped tbsp coarse mustard; salt and pepper.

Accompaniment

Puréed potatoes; onion purée (see recipe p. 171); chestnuts; red kidney beans, etc.

Trim off the fat and flatten the chops, to ensure they will cook evenly and not curl up at the sides. You can also use pork loin, Renoir's favorite: "Less chic, less presentable but more tender and juicy."

Leave to stand in a cool (but not too cold) place until the sauce is almost ready. Peel and finely chop the onions. Sauté gently in butter over a low heat. When the onions are transparent, pour in the white wine and reduce, always over a low heat and uncovered.

Meanwhile bring the stock to a boil in a saucepan, then turn down the heat and simmer, reducing the liquid by a third. Pour it over the onion and white wine mixture, stir with a spoon and leave to simmer for 5 to 7 minutes.

Rinse the gherkins and dry them. Then chop them and set aside on a piece of paper towel. Remove the sauce from the heat and add the mustard and chopped gherkins. Season to taste and keep warm.

If you have chosen puréed potatoes, you should begin their preparation at the same time as the sauce, finishing while the chops are frying. Puréed dishes do not like to stand around too long.

Season the chops and gently fry them in oil or fat for 5 to 6 minutes on each side. When cooked, place them on a rack over a plate. Cover and keep warm.

Heat a chafing dish and a large plate. Pour the purée into the dish and arrange the chops on the plate. Cover with sauce and serve immediately.

If there was not enough time to prepare a *charcutière*, Old Louise would make a sauce by adding stock to the frying pan, which was then reduced over a brisk heat, strained through a piece of cheesecloth, then spiced up with a dash of mustard, some chopped gherkins and a little chopped parsley.

BLANQUETTE DE VEAU À L'ANCIENNE
TRADITIONAL VEAL STEW

Madame Charigot, a seamstress by trade and soon to be Renoir's mother-in-law, used to frequent the kitchen of Madame Camille's little restaurant on Rue Saint-Georges, where Renoir often took his meals. She was a compatriot of the restaurant owner, and was already as renowned for her culinary talents as she was for her dressmaking. When Aline, her daughter, became Madame Renoir, she often used her mother's recipes.

For 6 people

3¹/₂lb veal (neck or shoulder); 1 bouquet garni; 1 celery stalk; 2 leeks, white parts only; 2 carrots; ¹/₂ lemon, peeled; 2 medium-sized onions, each studded with a clove; 2 quarts veal stock; salt and pepper.

Sauce

2 egg yolks; 1 cup extra-thick *crème fraîche* or heavy cream; 1 pinch grated nutmeg.

Garnish

¹/₂lb button mushrooms; ¹/₂lb pearl onions; ¹/₂ lemon; ¹/₄ cup butter; 2 fresh chervil sprigs.

Lamb or chicken are also suitable for this traditional stew recipe, as long as they have either soaked for 45 minutes in cold water (to which has been added the juice of half a lemon), or blanched for 3 minutes in cold water that is brought rapidly to a boil, and then skimmed, drained and rinsed.

Cut the meat into cubes, soak or blanch, then drain and pat dry. Place in a casserole that is just big enough to hold it. Add the bouquet garni, celery, leeks, carrots, peeled lemon and two clove-studded onions. Cover with veal stock and slowly bring to the boil. Carefully skim off the foam. Grease a large sheet of parchment paper. Place it over the ingredients and put the lid on the pot. Lower the heat and simmer gently for 25 minutes.

Meanwhile, clean the mushrooms and peel the pearl onions. Squeeze lemon juice over the mushrooms, and then fry them in 2 tablespoons of butter in a covered stainless steel saucepan over very low heat.

In another stainless steel saucepan, sauté the pearl onions in the remaining butter with a teaspoonful of lemon juice. Add salt and pepper, cover and reduce until the liquid disappears and they begin to caramelize.

When the veal is tender add the mushrooms and their juice, and the onions. Put the empty casserole aside, but don't wash it.

Draw off half the juice from the stew and strain it into the casserole. Cook over medium heat, uncovered.

In a bowl, beat the egg yolks with the cream. Add the grated nutmeg and some freshly ground pepper. Slowly beat in the reduced juice, and then pour the contents back into the saucepan and cook over a low heat, stirring all the time, until it thickens. Do not let it boil. When it has achieved a velvety thickness, place it in a double boiler.

Place the meat, mushrooms and onions on a well-heated serving dish. Strain the rest of the juice over the saucepan, and heat without boiling. Season to taste. Add a thin slice of peeled lemon, and mix well.

Pour the sauce over the serving dish, sprinkle with fresh chervil and serve immediately with a rice creole (see recipe p. 176).

DAUBE DE DINAN
DINAN'S RECIPE FOR BRAISED BEEF

For 6 people

2¹/₂ lb side of beef, chuck rib or rump; 4 medium-sized carrots; 4 medium-sized onions; 1 pint red wine from Provence; 1 cup cognac or marc; 6oz fatty pork rind; 4oz bacon; ¹/₂ cup olive oil; 4tbsp tomato purée; 3 cloves of garlic; salt and pepper.

Marinade

orange zest; 2 cloves; 1 sprig of thyme; 2 bay leaves; 6 ground peppercorns.

Prepare the meat a day ahead by cutting it into 12 or 15 pieces of roughly the same size. Put the meat in a terrine with one of the carrots, peeled and sliced, and two of the onions, peeled and chopped. Add the cloves, orange zest, thyme, bay leaves and pepper for the marinade, and splash liberally with wine and marc brandy (some chefs substitute good red wine vinegar for the marc and prefer dried orange rind to fresh as the flavor is more subtle).

Leave the covered terrine in the refrigerator overnight, stirring it once or twice. The next day, drain the meat in a colander positioned above a container to catch the juices.

You will need a large braising casserole or cooking pot with a lid. Cut the pork rind to fit the bottom of the casserole. Do not discard the leftover rind. Cut the bacon into strips, leaving on the rind.

Peel the rest of the onions and carrots, chop the onions and slice the carrots. Heat the oil in a large frying pan at medium heat.

Throw in the bacon and the chopped onions. Sauté until golden, stirring occasionally.

Place the well-drained meat on paper towels and pat dry. Take the onions and the bacon out of the pan, using a slotted spoon, and arrange them on top of the layer of pork rind.

Fry the beef cubes in the frying pan. If necessary, turn up the heat enough so that the meat browns nicely.

Pour the tomato purée into a large bowl. Strain the marinade through a colander, placing the bowl of tomato purée underneath to catch the juices. Stir. Make a bouquet garni with the aromatic ingredients and vegetables left in the colander by binding them with the discarded pork rinds in a piece of cheesecloth.

Preheat the oven to 350°F. Heat 1 pint of water in a saucepan. Using aluminum foil or parchment paper, cut out a circle that is larger than the lid of the braising casserole.

When the beef cubes are uniformly golden in color, take them out with a spatula and add them to the braising casserole with the bouquet garni, garlic and the carrot rounds. Sprinkle liberally with the tomato marinade and 1 cup of water. Add salt, fold the piece of parchment paper or aluminum foil over the top of the braising casserole and seal off completely with the lid.

Put it in the oven and lower the temperature to 350–375°F. Cook for 5 to 6 hours, gradually lowering the temperature to 325°F. Check the amount of liquid halfway through the cooking. Shake the droplets that form on the aluminum foil and the bottom of the lid back into the stew. If needed, add a little boiling water, or even better, some light stock (see recipe p. 159). Reseal with the

aluminum foil and the lid. Once the stew is cooked, remove the bouquet garni and arrange a layer of meats and vegetables (but no pork rind) on a warm platter. Cover with sauce and serve with thick macaroni.

The stew can also be served in cold, jellied slices and is best accompanied by a Provençale salad of cress, lamb's lettuce, lettuce, endive, dandelion leaves, chicory, fennel and fresh chervil.

GRIVES AU GENIEVRE
THRUSHES OR QUAILS IN JUNIPER SAUCE

This is yet another recipe from Dinan, whose fondness for animals often meant that he returned from hunting empty-handed. Nevertheless, he was always quite content to buy his game from a poacher.

For 6 people

6 thrushes, cleaned and plucked (if not available, substitute with quails); salt and freshly ground pepper; 12 juniper berries; 6 sprigs of fresh thyme; 6 thin slices of bacon, for barding; 3tbsp olive oil; 3tbsp stoned black olives.

Season the inside of each of the birds with pepper, a dash of salt, two crushed juniper berries and a tiny sprig of fresh thyme. Truss the birds and wrap a slice of bacon around each one. Use kitchen string to hold the bacon in place.

Heat the oil in a pot big enough to hold the six birds. Over a medium heat, sauté until golden brown on all sides. Season with salt and pepper, bearing in mind that the olives are already quite salty. Cover, reduce the heat and let cook for 10 minutes. Add the olives and leave to simmer for another 5 minutes, covered.

Take out the birds, remove their bacon wraps, and arrange them on a heated platter with a border of olives. Serve immediately with oven toasted or golden-fried slices of bread (it's best to use slightly stale bread).

If you wish to make a quick sauce, strain the oil and juices from the cooking pot through a damp, fine cheesecloth into a bowl. Glaze with chicken stock and reduce until almost entirely evaporated. Add some of the juices from the cooked birds and bring to the boil. Add a pinch of cayenne pepper and pour the sauce over the birds.

BŒUF MIROTON DE CAMILLE
CAMILLE'S BOILED BEEF

This is how Camille, the cream-maker, would concoct a dish from the left-over boiled beef. Another left-overs recipe which Renoir was fond of was a meat grill made from thickly cut pieces of beef, rolled first in the melted flavored fat from the pot-au-feu *(beef stew), then in cold* soubise *(onion purée) and lastly in breadcrumbs. Served with a* sauce ravigote *or simply with a good mustard, Renoir found this dish tasty and comforting.*

8tbsp onion purée (see recipe p. 171); 10 gherkins; 1 glass white wine vinegar or dry white wine; 2tbsp tomato purée; 4 parsley stalks; 5oz grated comté cheese; salt and pepper; approximately 1lb 5oz boiled beef; 1/4 cup butter.

Grease the bottom and sides of an oven-proof earthenware dish. Preheat the oven to 475°F.

Grease the bottom of a small saucepan and pour in the onion purée. Place on medium heat and let it warm up while you chop the gherkins into very thin rounds.

Add the gherkins to the onion purée together with the vinegar (or a good average white table wine). Stir the mixture and when it starts to bubble add the tomato purée (do not use tomato concentrate!), the finely chopped parsley and salt and pepper. Stir and let it reduce over low heat.

Grate the cheese and cut the boiled beef pieces into even slices.

Turn the heat off from under the sauce. Coat the bottom of the ovenproof dish with the sauce. Lay the sliced beef flat on the bottom and diagonally across the dish and coat with the sauce to cover seven-eighths of the meat, leaving the top almost completely covered (the dish must be quite deep).

Sprinkle with cheese and flakes of butter and place in the oven for 10 to 15 minutes. For this dish to be cooked to perfection the top must be brown and slightly crusty, and the meat very hot.

It can be served with rice, pasta shells or steamed potatoes (anything that will soak up well the slightly sharp sauce), along with a salad.

PIGEONNEAUX FARCIS
STUFFED PIGEONS

For 6 people

6 pigeons, their liver, gizzard and heart; 12 thinly cut slices of smoked bacon; 1tbsp butter; 1 cup dry white *banyuls* (a fortified wine); 6 shallots; 1/2 cup *crème fraîche* or heavy cream.

Stuffing

10 chicken livers; 2 shallots; 4oz Parma ham; 6 parsley stems; 1 cup fine champagne; 2tbsp onion purée (see recipe p. 171); 3 sage leaves; 1 pinch of ground juniper; salt and pepper; 2 large eggs.

Accompaniment

6 toasted slices of brioche

Use the pigeon livers whole (they do not hold any poisonous substance). Clean the gizzards and hearts and mince them together with the chicken livers (make sure to remove any green parts, they are poisonous), the

2 shallots, the ham and its fat, and the parsley. Mix the minced meat with white bread which has been soaked in fine champagne, the *soubise* purée, the remaining champagne, the finely chopped sage, ground juniper, salt, pepper and the eggs.

Season the cavity of the pigeons and stuff them, burying each pigeon liver at the center. Close and sew up the gap. Truss the birds, lay two bacon slices over their brisket and belly and bind with care. The pigeons are now ready for cooking and can be set aside, in a cool place, until needed.

Take a casserole just large enough to hold the pigeons. Peel the 6 shallots, keeping them whole (some chefs peel off the first layer of skin only, cooking the shallots "in their jacket", allowing the tender center to melt under the crusted skin).

Pre-heat the oven on 425°F. Place the casserole on a medium heat, melt the butter and lay the pigeons on to their side. Brown both sides of the brisket allowing the bacon to sizzle, then, using two spatulas (do not use any piercing or cutting utensil), turn them over. Let the top brown and only then fill the gaps with shallots.

After a few minutes, baste with *banyuls* (fortified wine), add salt and pepper, and seal the casserole firmly with a lid. Place in the oven to cook for 15 to 18 minutes, depending on the size of the birds. Baste once again 5 minutes before the end of cooking.

In the meantime, cut the brioche into slices and toast using a toaster or by laying them in a non-stick pan over medium heat.

As soon as the birds are cooked, remove them from the casserole and place each one on top of a toasted brioche slice, on a hot dish which had been set to warm in the switched-off oven.

Place the casserole over a high heat, strain some of the cooking liquid, remove the shallots and lay them on the dish. Pour the cream into the casserole, bring to a boil and let

it reduce slightly. Then coat the birds with this sauce.

Serve the pigeons accompanied with wild mushrooms, green peas or any vegetable that is in season.

PIECE DE BŒUF LARDÉE ET ROTIE
BACON-ROASTED JOINT OF BEEF

For 6 people

4oz smoked ham; ³/₄ cup armagnac, marc, or cognac; 1 thyme sprig; salt and freshly ground pepper; 3¹/₃lb cleaned joint of beef; 1tbsp grapeseed oil.

Sauce

1 large onion; 1 carrot; 1 shallot; 1 celery stalk; 3tbsp butter; 1 small glass of cognac; 1 bottle of Bouzy red wine or Ricey rosé; 1 half-trotter of veal; 2oz bacon rind; 1¹/₄lb beef or pork knuckle bones; 1 rosemary sprig (fresh if possible); 1 bouquet garni (made of parsley and small leek leaves); 1 quart veal stock; 1tbsp strong Dijon mustard; 1tbsp onion purée (see recipe p. 171); salt and freshly ground pepper.

Twenty-four hours in advance, prepare the beef: slice the ham into finger-sized pieces and soak them in the cognac, stripped thyme and a little pepper in a small bowl. Cover with a sheet of aluminum foil and leave for 2 hours in a cool (but not too cold) place. Ask your butcher to clean and remove the sinews from the piece of beef, if necessary. You could also ask him to stud it with the bacon slices and to tie it (not wrap it) in pork fat. If not, you could do it yourself, using a pointed knife or a skewer. Place the meat in a large basin or bowl, pour on the remaining marinade and brush with oil. Leave to marinate in a cool place for 24 hours.

You now have plenty of time to prepare a sauce. Here is one originating from the birthplace of Aline Renoir. Dice the onion, carrot, shallot and celery to make a *brunoise* (a sauce base). Sauté in the butter over a low heat for approximately 10 minutes. As soon as they begin to brown, glaze with the alcohol and flambé. Cover with the wine. Add the half-trotter, the rolled and tied bacon rind, the knuckle bones, the rosemary and the bouquet garni. Leave uncovered over a high heat until the liquid is reduced by about half.

Cover again with the veal stock, reduce the heat to medium and, without covering, leave to simmer for 15 minutes. Skim from time to time.

Turn off the heat, leave to stand for 8 to 10 minutes, then strain over a saucepan. Remove the bones, the half trotter, the rind and the bouquet garni. Using the back of a wooden spoon, gently press the remaining *brunoise* against the sides of a strainer in order to extract

the savory juices. Scrape the outside of the strainer to collect the pulp, put the saucepan over a low heat, add the Dijon mustard and stir well. Add the onion purée, stir again and leave until the consistency becomes rich and creamy.

Preheat the oven to 400–425°F.

Cook the oiled roast in an appropriately sized ovenproof dish for roughly 6 to 7 minutes per lb. Baste frequently with the cooking juices. Dust lightly with salt and freshly ground pepper.

Turn off the oven, wrap the roast in aluminum foil and leave to stand for 10 to 12 minutes, still inside the oven, the door ajar.

Carve the roast into slices and serve the sauce separately, piping hot in a warmed gravy boat. Accompany with *gâteau de pommes de terre* (see recipe p.176) or pilaf rice.

The plates should be warm, and the wine, a Bouzy for example, lightly chilled.

COTELETTES D'AGNEAU ONCLE HENRI

UNCLE HENRI'S LAMB CUTLETS

This was the favorite dish of uncle Henri and his wife Blanche. Renoir's eldest brother liked his food so much that he died after a copious meal while in "meditative digestion".

For 6 people

1 thyme sprig; 1 garlic clove; 2tbsp olive oil; 12 thick lamb cutlets; 1lb small potatoes; 6tbsp onion purée (see p. 171); salt and pepper; ground nutmeg; 1¹/₂ cups veal stock (see recipe p. 187); 3¹/₂tbsp butter.

For this recipe it is not necessary to use lean cutlets or prime chops. On the contrary, the lower ribs will be more tasty in a sauce.

Sprinkle thyme and stir the peeled and crushed garlic in the oil. Chop off the cutlet bones right at the edge of the meat, then leave the cutlets to marinate in the flavored oil for at least 2 hours (better results are achieved if they are left overnight). The cutlets should be turned around once or twice during the marinating time.

Grease with butter a deep ovenproof dish (earthenware or pyrex) big enough to hold all the cutlets.

Peel, rinse and pat dry the potatoes. Chop them up in rounds and blanch them for 10 minutes in salted boiling water.

Cook the stock over low heat and warm up the onion purée in a double boiler. Then preheat the oven to 400–425°F.

Remove the chops from the marinade and let the excess juice drip off then fry them, 3 minutes one side, 2 the other, in a non-stick frying pan over a high heat. Season the flipped side with pepper and a little salt. Pat dry with a paper towel and arrange them in the oven-proof dish.

Coat them in onion purée, then add a layer of potato rounds. Add pepper and ground nutmeg, but no salt. Coat once more with onion purée and top with another layer of potato mixed in the remaining onion purée. Sprinkle with ground nutmeg.

Baste with warm stock (do not use scalding hot stock!) and sprinkle on flakes of butter and braise for an hour. Then lower the heat to 300°F and leave to cook for another 30 minutes. Serve the lamb cutlets in the ovenproof dish.

Vegetables

GRATIN DE COURGETTES D'ALINE
ALINE'S BROILED ZUCCHINI

For 6 people

1¹/₂ lb small zucchini; 1 medium onion; 6 anchovy fillets in oil; 4tbsp olive oil; salt and freshly ground black pepper; 4 hard-boiled eggs; 2tbsp breadcrumbs; 1–1¹/₂tbsp butter.

Remove the ends from the zucchini but do not peel them, especially if they are small and young, so that they keep all their flavor. If you must peel them, use a vegetable slicer and remove only alternate slivers of skin.

Peel the onion and chop it coarsely. Cut the zucchini into thin slices and the anchovies into small pieces.

Heat 3 tablespoons of olive oil in a large frying pan. Toss the onion in and leave to brown, stirring occasionally with a wooden spoon. Once the onions are golden, add the anchovies, mix well, leave on the heat for 2 minutes, then throw in the zucchini.

Using a brush, lightly oil a baking dish. Pour the rest of the oil into the frying pan and carefully stir in the zucchini slices. The anchovies are already salty, so only salt lightly, but add a generous helping of freshly ground black pepper. Cook for 10 minutes over a low heat. Peel the hard-boiled eggs and break them up with a fork. Add them to the frying pan and stir the mixture.

Preheat the broiler. When it is hot, pour the contents of the frying pan into the baking dish and sprinkle with breadcrumbs and knobs of butter.

Place the dish under the broiler to brown.

Serve immediately, either as a light main dish or as an accompaniment to poached or broiled fish.

Traditionally, chopped garlic, parsley, fresh mint or cut basil are added to the ingredients in the frying pan. You can also substitute olive oil for the butter before putting it under the broiler.

TOMATES AU FOUR DE CÉZANNE
CÉZANNE'S BAKED TOMATOES

On the day her second son, Jean, was born, Madame Renoir asked her cook to prepare the dish described here. Though it is based on a recipe given to her by Cézanne, a close friend at the time, she did stipulate one thing: "Do be a little more generous with the olive oil." We have followed her example, knowing full well that Cézanne spoke only of a "little stream" or a "veil" of oil. Everyone present at the birth—at the time one still gave birth at home —so appreciated the dish (except Renoir himself, who was too worried to eat) that a second batch had to be made.

For 6 people

9 large tomatoes; 2tbsp table-salt; 4 garlic cloves; 1 bouquet garni of parsley; freshly ground black pepper; 4tbsp olive oil; 3tbsp breadcrumbs.

Wash and dry the tomatoes then cut them in half lengthwise. Salt abundantly on the cut surface and lay them, salt side down, on a rack over a dish to allow to drain. After 10 minutes, squeeze them delicately between the fingers to remove any excess water and seeds.

Preheat the oven to 425°F. Using a pastry brush, brush a baking dish with oil. The dish should be large enough to hold all the 18 tomato halves.

Peel, crush and finely chop the garlic. Remove the parsley leaves from their stalks and chop them finely. Mix the garlic and parsley with the pepper to make the *persillade* (a mix of crushed garlic and chopped parsley). Arrange the tomato halves inside the dish. With a knife, spread a coating of *persillade* over each tomato half, then pour on a generous helping of oil and sprinkle with the breadcrumbs. Bake for 20 to 25 minutes, keeping a watchful eye to avoid burning. If you think it necessary, you can use the broiler to crisp the tops.

PURÉE SOUBISE
ONION PURÉE

For 6 people

12 large onions; 3tbsp short-grain rice; 1 pint chicken stock; 2tbsp heavy cream; 1 heaped tbsp softened butter; 1 pinch table salt, coarse salt, white pepper and grated nutmeg.

Chop the onions finely and blanch for 6 minutes in water salted with coarse salt. Drain and transfer to a heavy-based enamel pot. Add the rice and chicken stock and top up with water. Cover the pot with parchment paper, buttered side down, so the edges of the paper hang over the sides of the pot, and put the lid on.

The best way to prepare this dish is in a preheated oven, at a medium temperature for 50 minutes. You can also cook it over a very low heat on the stove. Dampen a thick dish cloth, twist it into a turban and use it to cover the lid. Cook for 30 minutes. Check to make sure there is still liquid in the pot, moisten the turban and cook for another 10 minutes, or until the rice and onions are completely done. Uncover and leave on the heat for another 5 minutes. Pass through a strainer to eliminate all moisture, and then blend in a food processor or mixer until puréed.

Rinse and dry the pot and pour in the purée. Return to low heat. Stir in the cream first, and then the butter. When everything is well-blended add a pinch of nutmeg, and salt and pepper to taste.

This dish was well-known at the beginning of this century in France, either as an accompaniment to grilled meat or, with extra cream, butter or dripping, as a sauce. It was also often used with rice instead of béchamel sauce, with egg yolk added to make the dish even richer.

POIS MANGE-TOUT AUX GRELONS
YOUNG SNOW PEAS
WITH BACON

When Renoir feasted at Essoyes in the early spring, he took full advantage of the varieties of tender snow peas that were grown locally, like "crochus rois des gourmands" and "fondants de Saint-Désirat". These were often prepared with "grêlons", little cubes of crisp-fried bacon.

For 6 people

7oz bacon; 1lb 10oz snow peas; 3 sprigs parsley; 2 lettuce hearts; 6 scallions; $^1/_2$ cup + 1tbsp butter; 1 pinch sugar (optional); 1 sprig tarragon; salt and freshly ground black pepper.

Trim the fat from the bacon, cut into small pieces and gently fry over a medium heat in a non-stick frying pan until they brown, while stirring continuously with a wooden spoon.

Clean and trim the snow peas, removing both ends and all filaments. Drop them whole in a large stainless steel pot along with the stripped parsley, lettuce hearts, cleaned and cut into three parts, whole onions, butter, and $^1/_2$ cup of still mineral water. Don't add any salt yet, and only add sugar if the snow peas are not young and fresh.

Cover and place over a medium heat. When it starts to boil, lower the heat and leave to simmer for 7 to 8 minutes. Season lightly.

Remove the bacon pieces from the pan and place on paper towels to absorb the grease. Pat them completely dry and add them to the pot. Simmer for another 2 minutes.

Strip the tarragon leaves and sprinkle over the snow peas and bacon. Add salt and pepper to taste and serve immediately in a heated shallow dish.

For a more extravagant touch, put melted *crème fraîche* flavored with a tiny dash of grated nutmeg into this dish, and then serve it with croûtons pan-fried in bacon fat.

HARICOTS ROUGES AU LARD
RED KIDNEY BEANS
WITH SMOKED BACON

The red beans purchased from Camille, who ran the dairy on the Rue Saint-George, did not need soaking for very long. They came directly from Dijon and were real *haricots de vignes*, grown on rough, stony ground between rows of *cèpe* mushrooms.

For 6 people

1$^1/_4$lb red kidney beans; 12oz smoked bacon; 1 bouquet garni (2 sage leaves, fresh parsley and small celery stalks and 1 clove); 2 large onions; 1 clove garlic; 1 red pepper; 1$^3/_4$ cups red burgundy; 6oz sausage meat; $^1/_2$tsp paprika; salt and pepper.

Soak the beans in fresh cold water (not too cold). A few hours should suffice.

Remove the rind from the bacon and tie it together with the other ingredients for the bouquet garni. Slice the bacon into finger-sized slivers.

Drain the kidney beans, rinse and drain again. Put them in a large cast iron pot with the bacon, the bouquet garni, the chopped onions and garlic and the red pepper.

Pour in the red wine and add water so that the liquid covers the ingredients by $^3/_4$ inch.

Cover three-quarters of the pot with the lid and bring gently to the boil. Skim the liquid regularly until it is clear, then close the lid completely. Simmer for approximately 1 hour.

Take the sausage meat and press it into a pancake shape with a fork. Heat a non-stick frying pan. Lay the sausage meat "pancake" in the pan and fry gently while pressing with a spatula. Turn it over using another spatula taking care not to break it up.

Once the sausage meat has lost its fat, remove the meat and dry it on a piece of paper towel. Discard the fat in the frying pan and clean it out with paper towels.

Put the frying pan over a low heat and place the sausage meat "pancake" in it. Lightly sprinkle it with paprika. Season with salt and pepper and pour over two ladlefuls of stock from the kidney beans.

Leave to cook gently, breaking up the meat with a wooden spoon as it cooks. Put the mixture into a saucepan on a low heat, stir again, cover and leave to simmer for 40 minutes. Meanwhile, prepare some croûtons.

Pour the contents into a large shallow dish and serve the croûtons separately. A crisp salad well tossed in a Dijon mustard vinaigrette makes a perfect accompaniment to this feast from Burgundy.

LES FARCIS MAIGRES DE LÉGUMES
LEAN STUFFED VEGETABLES

For 6 people

6 eggplants, zucchini or tomatoes; 4tbsp olive oil; 3 large onions; 6 cloves of garlic; 2 green peppers; 3oz fresh mushrooms, or 1$^1/_2$oz dried mushrooms; 2 egg-sized balls of stale breadcrumbs; 1 oregano or savory sprig; 2 sprigs of parsley; 1 basil sprig; salt and freshly ground pepper; 4 anchovies (optional).

Choose plump vegetables rather than long thin ones. Remove the stalks from the eggplants or zucchini. Cut the vegetables in half lengthwise and, using a small spoon, remove the flesh from the inside and set aside for later. If you are using tomatoes, slice off the top, scoop out the insides and drain them in a colander.

In a frying pan, heat 2 tablespoons of oil and toss in the onion and the chopped garlic. Leave them to soften over a medium heat. Pour 1 tablespoon of oil into a flameproof baking dish and lay the vegetables in it, cut face up. Put the dish over a low heat, half cover and leave the vegetables to soften.

When the onions and garlic are lightly golden, add the mashed or chopped flesh from the vegetables (if using tomatoes, avoid adding the seeds) then the finely chopped peppers and the cleaned and dried mushrooms, thinly chopped. As these ingredients give off a lot of water, don't cover the dish, but allow the juice to evaporate. When the mixture resembles a purée, add the stale bread to absorb the remaining liquid. Remove from the heat and leave to cool before transferring to a bowl.

Meanwhile, remove the oregano, parsley and basil leaves from their stems and cut them up with scissors. Mix the herbs and vegetables in a bowl, and add salt and pepper to taste. Anchovies can also be added, but they must be free of bones and de-salted (see the recipe for *anchoïade* on p. 142 — in fact the paste can be used in this recipe). Chop, mash and incorporate them into the stuffing. Taste before adding salt.

Preheat the oven to 350°F.

Stuff the vegetables with the mixture. Put them in a baking dish, sprinkle with the remaining olive oil and cook for 20 to 25 minutes. Baste once or twice during cooking with the juice from the vegetables, spooning it while carefully tipping the dish. Once cooked, turn off the heat and leave to sit in the oven with the door slightly ajar for another 5 minutes.

Serve as a starter, or as an accompaniment to lamb chops.

Variation on the stuffing: instead of anchovies, you can add 6oz of chopped Parma ham in slices. Take care not to add too much salt, as the dish will become saltier during cooking.

BROUILLADE AUX LÉGUMES
MIXED VEGETABLE DISH

For 6 people

10oz ham (1 thick slice); 3³/₄lb young fava beans, shelled; 1 bunch small scallions; 2 bundles asparagus; 18 small purple artichokes; 1 lemon; 1 large onion, peeled and diced; 1 medium-sized carrot, peeled and diced; 3tbsp olive oil; 1 cup Côte de Provence white wine; 4 unpeeled cloves of garlic; salt and pepper; 1tsp fennel seeds.

Cut the thick slice of ham into long strips, leaving the fat on. It will dissolve while cooking, enhancing the flavor of the meat and lending it a rich golden color.

Place the shelled fava beans in boiling water for 20 seconds to remove their inner skin. Trim the scallions, leaving 1¹/₂–1³/₄ inches of the green part.

Trim the asparagus and cut them diagonally into ³/₄ inch long pieces. Leave the asparagus tips in one piece even if some are longer than ³/₄ inch and keep them separate from the rest of the asparagus pieces.

Trim the artichoke leaves by cutting off about 1 inch from the tip, depending on the size of each leaf. Remove the little leaves attached to the artichoke stem, as well as the outer leaves at its base. With a vegetable peeler, peel the stem until you reach the thin, white, tender heart. Split the artichokes into 4 pieces and rub the insides with half a lemon. This prevents them turning brown. Do not squeeze all the juice out of the lemon as it will be used again later. Peel the large onion and the carrot and chop them up finely.

In a large frying pan, heat the oil over a medium heat. Add the strips of ham and fry for

3 minutes, until golden on each side. Take out the ham and keep it warm between two plates, using one turned upside down as a lid. Gently fry the diced onion and carrot into the pan for 5 minutes. Stir frequently, so that the onion turns golden but does not brown.

Add the artichokes and white wine. Squeeze the remaining juice out of the lemon and pour it into the pan. Cook for 10 minutes. Throw in the scallions and garlic. After 5 minutes, add the asparagus pieces, but not the tips. Stir continuously for 6 or 7 minutes. Add the asparagus tips. Salt and pepper to taste and after 2 minutes, put in the fava beans, stirring gently.

Sprinkle with fennel seeds, and allow to cook for 5 minutes, uncovered, over a low heat. Stir in the strips of ham and continue cooking for another minute. Serve on a heated serving platter.

GATEAU DE POMMES DE TERRE
POTATO CAKE

For 6 people

2¹/₄lb medium-sized potatoes; 2tbsp goose fat or butter; finely
ground sea salt and freshly ground black pepper.

Preheat the oven to 400°F. Choose evenly
sized potatoes for an attractive presentation,
then wash, peel and quickly rinse them. Dry
and cut them into very thin slices, no thicker
than ¹/₁₆ inch.

In a very large frying pan, melt half the
goose fat or butter. Make a layer of as many
slices of potato as possible, overlapping them if
necessary. As the potatoes were only lightly
washed, the starch in them will bind them
together, until they are a golden brown.

Take a large flat plate and turn the cake
out on to it by covering the frying pan with the
plate and inverting them with a brisk
movement. Slide the cake back into the frying
pan, golden side up. Sprinkle it with salt and
pepper and leave until lightly golden.

Choose a deep, round oven dish large
enough to hold the cake. Slide the cake into the
dish and put it in the oven, lowering the heat
to 300–350°F.

Repeat all the previous steps a second
and third time to obtain as many layers as the
dish can hold. Once you have added the last
layer, leave the dish in the oven for 10 more
minutes. Serve by turning the cake out onto a
large warm plate or slide it using two spatulas.
Sprinkle with fresh finely chopped parsley (add
chopped garlic if you are serving it with lamb
or pork) and a light sprinkling of freshly
ground pepper.

RIZ À LA CRÉOLE DE VOLLARD
VOLLARD'S CREOLE RICE

For 6 people

1 medium-sized onion; 2tbsp butter; 1tbsp olive oil; 1 fennel
sprig; 1 thyme sprig; 1 medium-sized bowl of rice; 2¹/₂
medium-sized bowls beef or chicken stock; salt and pepper;
1 fresh bay leaf.

Peel and finely chop the onion. Put half
the butter and the olive oil into a shallow
flameproof oven dish and melt over a low heat.
When the butter and oil are suf-ficiently hot,
toss in the chopped onions and slowly cook
until transparent. Heat the stock with all the
herbs except the bay leaf.

Preheat the oven to 475°F. Combine the
rice with the onion and stir with a wooden
spoon until each grain of rice is transparent.
Wet the rice with the stock (and its herbs),
add salt (preferably rock salt), and freshly
ground pepper and turn up the heat until the
mixture comes to a rapid boil. Add the bay
leaf, place the dish in the oven and bake for 15
to 20 minutes.

Turn the heat off and add to the rice—
which should by now have absorbed all the
liquid—the remaining butter, cut into small
pieces. Leave the dish in the oven with the heat
off and the door partially open until the butter
has been completely absorbed into the rice
(about 2 to 3 minutes). Remove the herbs and
serve immediately.

Madame Renoir adored this way of cooking rice
to perfection and insisted that Vollard gave her
the recipe.

Desserts

TARTE AUX FIGUES
FIG TART

For 6 people

20oz shortcrust pastry; 1³/₄lb fresh figs; 1tsp grated lemon
rind; 1 cup Côtes-de-Provence red wine; ²/₃ cup brown
sugar, plus 2tbsp more for the final frosting; ¹/₄ cup dark
raisins; 1 small glass dark rum; ¹/₃ cup soft brown sugar;
¹/₂ cup ground almonds; 1tsp ground cinnamon.

Roll out the dough on a flat surface and
grease a deep cake pan, paying special attention
to where the sides meet the bottom. Line the tin
with the dough and leave to stand at room
temperature for 30 minutes.

Wash and dry the figs. Cut ¹/₂ inch from
the stem—the white part of the fruit is bitter.
Choose a small stainless steel saucepan and
arrange the figs in rows, without leaving any
gaps. Add the lemon rind and pour the red
wine over the figs, sprinkle with sugar and
place over a low heat. Poach for 15 minutes.

Preheat the oven to 450°F. Put the
raisins in water and bring to the boil. Leave
them to soak in the water for 5 minutes. Drain
and soak in rum.

In a bowl, mix the soft brown sugar,
ground almonds and cinnamon with just

enough of the rum from the raisins to form a
thick paste.

Pre-bake the dough for 10 minutes in the
oven, remove and spread evenly and rapidly
with the almond paste. Return to the oven and
lower the temperature to 350°F.

While the dough is browning, carefully
remove the figs from the wine, which by now
should be very syrupy. Place them one by one
on a large serving dish. Halve them lengthwise.

Take out the tart. Arrange the halved figs
inside the tart with their cut sides facing up to
form a flower petal pattern. Sprinkle with the
remaining 2 tablespoons of sugar mixed with a
little cinnamon and the raisins. Bake for 10 to
12 more minutes.

GATEAU AU CHOCOLATE
CHOCOLATE CAKE

For 6 to 8 people

Sponge cakes

12 tablespoons soft butter; 2 cups flour; 1¹/₂ cups sugar;
1¹/₂lb bittersweet chocolate; 4tbsp very strong coffee; 10
eggs; 1 pinch of salt.

Filling

14oz sweet chocolate; ¹/₂lb bittersweet chocolate; ¹/₄ cup
thick *crème fraîche* or heavy cream.

Frosting

3tbsp apricot preserves, diluted with water and strained;
³/₄lb bittersweet chocolate; 3tbsp groundnut oil.

Decoration

1 cup chocolate shavings.

Begin by making the chocolate sponge cakes. You can halve the ingredients and make one cake at a time or, if you prefer, order them from a good bakery. In either case, they should sit for 24 hours before being cut.

Carefully grease two 8 inch square cake pans with butter. Lightly flour them, turning them over and tapping them on the bottom to get rid of excess flour. Put them in the refrigerator. Break up the chocolate and toss the pieces into a double boiler at low heat. Add the coffee and let the mixture melt, without stirring. Once melted, smooth it over with a spoon.

In a large bowl, mix together the rest of the butter and sugar. Crack the eggs and separate the whites from the yolks. Beat the yolks, one by one, into the butter and sugar mixture. Work in the rest of the flour.

Preheat the oven to 350°F. Pour the melted chocolate into the butter, yolk and sugar mixture and stir until the texture is well blended. Whisk the egg whites with a pinch of salt until they form peaks. Whisk a spoonful of the stiff egg whites into the other mixture. Then, delicately but thoroughly, fold in the rest of the whites.

Take the pans out of the refrigerator and pour in the mixture, smoothing the surface with a spoon. Bake for 30–35 minutes. Test to see if the cakes are ready by pricking the center of each cake with the tip of a knife. They are done when the blade comes out clean.

To prepare the two fillings, pour half of the cream into a heavy-based saucepan and bring to a rapid boil. Take the saucepan off the heat and add the pieces of sweet chocolate. Beat the mixture until smooth. Allow it to cool, but not harden. Repeat the same procedure with the bittersweet chocolate filling.

To assemble the cakes, cut each sponge cake into 2 identical layers with a bread knife. Spread sweet chocolate on 2 of the squares and bittersweet chocolate on the bottom half of the remaining squares. Stack one on top of the other, alternating between dark and light chocolate, and finishing with the uncovered top piece. Lightly press the layers together to make them stick together.

For the frosting, use a small brush to spread the diluted apricot preserves, which you should warm slightly, on the top of the cake. In a double boiler, melt the chocolate. Take the double boiler off the heat, add the groundnut oil and stir again. Pour the frosting on to the cake, and with a long spatula, ease it over the

sides. Smooth the surfaces with a serrated knife. Decorate by arranging a bow shape from chocolate shavings.

TARTE AUX PETITS FRUITS ROUGES
RED BERRY TART

Enormous pies and tarts filled with seasonal fruits and berries were baked all year round in the bread oven at Essoyes.

For 6 people

1lb shortcrust flan pastry (for a 10–12 inch pie dish); 2 pints medium-sized strawberries; $^{1}/_{2}$ lemon; $^{1}/_{4}$ cup sugar; butter; 1 pint red berries (wild strawberries, raspberries, redcurrants; whatever is in season); 3tbsp redcurrant or raspberry jelly; whipped cream; fresh mint leaves.

If you make your own pastry, roll it into a ball and let it rest for at least 1 hour in the refrigerator before using. The longer it rests the less it will need to be pre-baked.

Clean the strawberries by running them swiftly under running water in a strainer. Dry, hull, and place in a large mixing bowl. Squeeze lemon juice over the fruit, sprinkle it with sugar and put it in the refrigerator for 30 minutes. Meanwhile, clean and prepare the other berries.

Carefully grease the inside of the pie dish and chill it in the refrigerator. Cut a piece of aluminum foil or parchment paper to fit the base of the dish. Preheat the oven to 425–450°F.

Lightly flour your work surface, pastry roller and hands. Flatten the pastry and roll it out lightly to a thickness of approximately $^{1}/_{4}$ inch. Do not overwork the pastry, which is extremely fragile and will easily fall to pieces. Remove the pie dish from the refrigerator and line with pastry. Use your fingertips to fit the pastry snugly over the entire surface of the dish. Cut off the excess pastry, prick with a fork, cover with the circle of paper or foil, and fill with small stones or dried beans (these will keep the pastry from puffing up in the oven). Pre-bake the pastry for 20 minutes.

Heat the jelly in a saucepan, but do not let it boil.

Drain the strawberries and reserve the juice. Halve them lengthwise.

Take the pastry case out of the oven; take out the paper and beans and set it aside to cool. While still slightly warm, very carefully remove the pastry from the dish. Arrange the strawberry halves in a circle around the inside edge of the pastry case. Arrange the other berries in the center.

Mix the juice and jelly together; cover the berries, using a pastry brush.

Serve with whipped cream and decorate with fresh mint leaves.

This tart can also be made with flaky puff pastry or sweet crumbly pastry. Only use shortcrust pastry with apples, quinces, pears, plums, or any other fruit that is cooked inside the pie dish at the same time as the pastry.

GELÉE D'ORANGES
DES COLLETTES
ORANGE PRESERVE
FROM LES COLLETTES

For 6 people

4¹/₂ lb apples; 10 unwaxed oranges; 6³/₄ cups sugar.

Carefully scrub the apples and, without peeling, cut each into 8 sections. Place the apple pieces with seeds into a stainless steel saucepan and cover with 5 cups of water. Cook uncovered over a low heat until they begin to come apart. Allow to cool completely and drain over a bowl. Set the collected juice aside.

Wash and dry the oranges and peel off the rind. Remove as much of the pith as possible; you only need to use the zest.Cut the orange zest into strips; cut the oranges in half and squeeze their juice. Tie the seeds up in a small cheesecloth bundle.

Place the sugar and 2 quarts of the cooked apple juice in a large pot. Heat to 217°F, or until the syrup becomes smooth and glossy. If you do not have a thermometer, keep a close eye on the syrup. When small bubbles form on the surface and a small spoonful of syrup held under cold water forms a ball you can roll between your fingers, it is ready to be removed from the heat.

Gently press the apple pieces to extract all of their juice. Strain the juice. Add the apple juice, orange zest, and bag of orange seeds to the syrup. Bring slowly to the boil, reduce to a simmer and cook for 25 minutes.

Sterilize jam jars, and set them out in a row. Fill with hot, but not boiling, jelly, a little at a time, so as to allow the glass to warm gradually. Leave them in an unheated oven at room temperature until they completely cool down, then refrigerate for 8 hours. Cover the surface of the preserve with wax paper that has been sprinkled with a drop of marc. Cover the top of the jar with thick paper and fasten with string.

This preserve goes very well with custards, charlottes and tarts.

CREME À LA VANILLE
ET AU CARAMEL
VANILLA CARAMEL CUSTARD

For 6 people

1 vanilla bean; 1quart whole milk; 8 egg yolks; 4 eggs; 1³/₄ cups sugar; 1tsp butter.

Caramel

²/₃ cup sugar; ¹/₂tsp lemon juice; 1¹/₂tbsp water.

Split the vanilla bean lengthwise into quarters, without detaching the strips from the stem. Slowly simmer the milk. Add the vanilla bean. Leave to cool completely before removing the vanilla. Rinse and dry the vanilla bean, as it can be used again.

Break the eggs in a large bowl, removing all traces of the albumen. Add the sugar and blend with a whisk until smooth and creamy. Pour in the milk, a little at time, whisking constantly.

Preheat the oven to 400°F/. Butter the inside of a mold and refrigerate.

Prepare the caramel (see recipe p. 189). Remove the mold from the refrigerator and pour in enough caramel to cover the bottom. Rotate the mold so as to completely cover it with caramel. Now fill the mold with custard to within 1 inch of the top. Half-fill a large water-bath with water and place the mold inside. Bake in the oven for 30 minutes. To ensure that the water in the water-bath does not boil over into the custard, add one or two ice cubes, or some ice cold water.

Remove the custard and allow to cool before carefully turning it out on to a shallow serving plate.

You can also make individual caramel custards in small earthenware dishes (rame-kins). To make a chocolate custard add 4oz of bittersweet chocolate. For a coffee-flavored custard add 2 teaspoons of instant coffee, and if you like pralines, as did Madame Charigot, Renoir's mother-in-law, add in a small handful.

BOURDELOTS ET DOUILLONS
APPLE AND PEAR PASTRIES

Renoir loved all fruits and desserts, but he was especially fond of bourdelots—*whole apples and pears wrapped in pastry—as they reminded him of his very happy stay with the Bérards at their manor in Wargemont, near Dieppe. The house was overflowing with children, and Renoir painted many of their portraits, and took part in all of their games and tea parties.*

For 6 people

1lb shortcrust pastry; 6 large apples or pears; $^3/_4$ cup + 2tbsp butter; 6tbsp sugar; 1 small glass calvados; $^1/_2$tsp cinnamon; 1 egg yolk; 3tbsp milk, heated then cooled.

Roll out the pastry and place the apples or pears on it lengthwise. Cut the pastry into 6 squares, making sure that each one is big enough to completely envelop its piece of fruit.

Peel and core the fruit, leaving them whole. Cream the butter in a bowl and blend in the sugar until smooth. Mix in the calvados and cinnamon. Stuff the mixture into the core of the fruit with a spatula.

Preheat the oven to 475°F. Stand an apple or pear in the center of each pastry square. Take all 4 corners of the pastry square and join at the top sealing the pastry by pinching together the edges tight with moistened fingertips.

Beat the egg yolk and stir in the cold milk. Brush evenly over the wrapped fruit. Cut out small leaf shapes from some of the unused dough. Fix to the tops of each pastry with egg yolk. Arrange on a lightly buttered baking sheet and cook for 30 minutes. If the pastries appear to be changing colour too dramatically, lower the temperature to 425°F. Serve hot or cold with *crème fraîche*.

DIPLOMATE BELLE EPOQUE
DIPLOMAT SPONGE CUSTARD

For 6 people

10oz candied fruit; 8 egg yolks; 1 cup sugar; ³/₄ cup light cream; 1¹/₂tsp cornflour; 6 sheets of gelatin; 1¹/₂tbsp unsalted butter; ³/₄ cup corn syrup; 7oz lady fingers; whipping cream or Italian meringue; 2oz crystallized violet petals or 4oz decorative sugar pearls or silver balls.

Chop the candied fruit and soak it in Grand Marnier or rum.

To prepare the custard, beat the egg yolks and sugar in a mixing bowl until light yellow. Add the cream and mix together well. Stir the cornflour into a glass of cold water and add to the mixture.

Soften the gelatin leaves in cold water.

Half-fill a large saucepan (big enough to hold the mixing bowl containing the custard mixture) with cold water and place over a medium heat. Place the mixing bowl inside to form a double boiler and stir with a wooden spoon until the custard begins to thicken. Remove from the heat and continue stirring for a few more seconds. Drain the gelatin and stir into the custard.

Butter a 2 quart charlotte mould. Then drain the candied fruit, and slowly pour the corn syrup into the leftover liqueur.

Cut one end off 20 lady fingers. When they are squeezed together tightly, there should be just enough to line the walls of the mold. Cut another 12 into pointed pieces for the bottom of the mold. Don't throw away the leftover pieces.

Soak all parts of the sponge fingers in the syrup-liqueur mixture. Arrange the pointed pieces in a rosette pattern on the bottom of the mold. Line the walls with the other pieces, with their cut ends facing up.

Alternate layers of warm custard with layers of candied fruit until the mould is half-full. Cover with a layer of soaked lady finger ends, then continue alternating layers of custard and fruit until you reach the top of the mold. Cover with another layer of soaked lady fingers, making sure that the entire surface is well sealed.

Cover with plastic wrap and fit a piece of heavy cardboard or wood over the surface. Place a weighted object on top and refrigerate for 6 to 8 hours.

Turn out the *diplomat* on to a serving dish and decorate with whipping cream or Italian meringue, using an icing nozzle or pastry bag. Decorate with crystallized violet petals or, if you prefer, sugar pearls and silver balls.

TARTE AU POTIRON
PUMPKIN PIE

For 6 people

2¹/₂ lb pumpkin or red squash; 1lb shortcrust pastry, infused with a few drops orange-blossom water; 2tbsp olive oil; ¹/₂ cup granulated sugar; 3tbsp butter; 1tbsp orange-blossom water, elderberry brandy or fruit brandy; salt.

Cut the pumpkin into quarters and remove the skin and seeds. Cut the flesh into small cubes. Cook, preferably by steaming until tender, then drain in a colander.

Roll out the pastry into a 12-inch circle (for a 10-inch cake pan) and lightly brush with olive oil. Butter the cake pan, using liberal amounts of butter in the corners, where the bottom meets the sides (use a springform pan, as this is an extremely fragile pie). Line the cake pan with pastry and secure firmly at the edges by pinching the dough with your fingers. Leave to stand.

Preheat the oven to 425°F. Purée the pumpkin flesh in a food processor. Pour into a mixing bowl. Add sugar and butter while beating to a purée with a wooden spoon. Add the orange-blossom water or brandy.

Roll out the leftover pastry into rectangles and cut into ¹/₂ inch strips long enough to cover the surface of the pie.

Fill the pastry shell with the puréed pumpkin and arrange the pastry strips in a lattice on the top.

Place the pie in the oven and bake for 30 to 40 minutes.

You can serve this dish hot or warm, unaccompanied or with whipped cream or vanilla ice-cream.

Renoir often treated himself to this dessert, which he would sprinkle liberally with a good Pinot rosé wine.

RIZ À L'IMPÉRATRICE
EMPRESS RICE PUDDING

For 6 people

1¹/₄ cups candied fruit; 1 cup rum or kirsch; 2 cups round-grain rice; 1¹/₄ cups sugar; 1 vanilla bean; 2tbsp butter; 1¹/₂ pints whole milk; 6 egg yolks; 6 gelatin leaves; 1²/₃ cups *crème fraîche* or heavy cream.

Dice the candied fruit. Pour the rum or kirsch into a small bowl, adding all the fruit, less one spoonful to be used for final decoration. Mix together, cover the bowl with plastic wrap and leave to soak at room temperature while you prepare the rice.

In a large pot bring 1 quart of water to the boil. Pour in the rice. Cook uncovered for 5 minutes. Strain and rinse under cold running water and strain again.

Place a saucepan in a double boiler, add ¹/₃ cup of sugar, the vanilla bean, butter and 1¹/₄ cups of milk. Simmer over a medium heat, making sure it does not bubble, for 5 minutes, stirring occasionally.

Add the well-drained rice and mix. Cover and cook over a low heat for 25 minutes. The rice is cooked once all the milk has been absorbed.

Pour the rice into an earthenware baking dish, add the fruit and alcohol syrup and mix gently with a fork. Leave to cool at room temperature.

Prepare the egg custard (see recipe p. 188). Soften the gelatin leaves in cold water, drain, and add to the still warm egg custard. Pour over the rice and stir with a fork.

Whisk the heavy cream or *crème fraîche*, thinned with a spoonful or two of milk to give it a firm but light texture. Mix the cream into the rice.

Lightly grease a sponge cake pan with oil. Fill with the rice mixture and cover with plastic wrap. Refrigerate for at least 6 hours, or overnight, if possible.

To loosen the pudding, briefly dip the bottom of the cake pan in hot water before turning the pudding out on to a chilled plate.

Decorate the pudding with the remaining candied fruit and serve it with a sauce made from either strawberry, blackcurrant or redcurrant preserve which has been diluted with a little warm water.

Stocks and Sauces

NAGE POUR CRUSTACÉS OU POISSONS
FISH OR SHELLFISH STOCK

This stock is to be used when preparing seafood or fish. The basic ingredients for the stock are vegetables, herbs and spices and wine. When either the fish bones or crustacean shells are added to it, the nage (fish stock) then becomes a fumet (fish bisque).

Makes 3 quarts

1 white onion; 1 carrot; 1 leek; 1 celery stalk; 1 bouquet garni with parsley stalks; 1tsp black peppercorns; 2 garlic cloves; celery leaves and dark green leek leaves; unwaxed lemon rind; 1tsp coriander or fennel seeds; $1/2$ unwaxed lemon or 1tbsp white wine vinegar; 1 pint dry white wine.

Clean, peel and rinse the vegetables. Chop them up and drop them in a cooking pot containing 3 quarts of water. Add the bouquet garni and seasoning. Place over a high heat and bring to the boil.

Cover and lower the heat. Let it simmer for 20 minutes. Skim off the foam, as vegetables always give out some impurities. Add the vinegar and the wine and cook for about 10 more minutes. Then allow to cool and strain.

At this point the shells or fish bones can be poached so as to flavor the stock, which will later on be used to make the *fumet*.

FUMET
FISH OR SHELLFISH BISQUE

Makes $1^1/2$ quarts

1 medium-sized shallot; 1 onion; 4oz button mushrooms; 2tbsp olive oil; 2 $1/4$ lb white fish bones (bones and heads without the gills), or crustacean shells and head; 1 glass dry white wine; $5^1/2$ pints fish stock.

Peel and clean the vegetables. Cut off the mushroom ends. Pour the oil into a stewing pot and heat up gently. Throw in the vegetables and cook them for 5 minutes. Add the pulverized crustacean shells or fish bones. While stirring, increase the heat and simmer for 5 to 7 minutes.

Pour in the wine and leave to boil for 20 seconds so that the alcohol may evaporate, reducing the acidity. Lower the heat and pour in $5^1/2$ pints of fish stock, after having strained it. Simmer for 25 to 30 minutes. Turn off the heat and allow to cool completely.

Take a strainer, put a piece of damp cheesecloth on the bottom and put it on a mixing bowl. Then strain the stock through, using a ladle and taking care not to press any solids through.

The *fumet* can keep for 4 days in the refrigerator or a few weeks in the freezer. The same stock can be made from crab, crayfish or shrimp shells.

These stocks are used for cooking but they can also be served as sauces or cream soups.

BOUILLON DE VEAU
VEAL STOCK

The basic ingredients are the same as for the poultry stock: vegetables, herbs and spices, and wine. Purchase 4¹/₂lb of veal knuckle or neck bones, broken into small pieces. Toss the bones in cold water and heat up. Regularly skim off the foam and add the vegetables, seasoning and wine. Leave to simmer over a low heat for 3 hours. Then strain the stock.

BOUILLON DE VOLAILLE
POULTRY STOCK

For 3 quarts of stock

4¹/₂lb of poultry giblets (neck, wings, feet, carcass); 2 of each of the vegetables used for the fish stock (recipe p. 186) except for fennel; 2 more garlic cloves; 1 bouquet garni; 1 small piece of fresh root ginger, thinly chopped; 1 glass (about ³/₄ cup) of dry white wine or sparkling apple cider; coarse salt; white pepper.

Clean the giblets, cut off the claws from the feet and the beak if the head is to be used. Rinse thoroughly and take out the cartilage from the neck. Blanch the feet and remove the skin, which should come off easily.

Hold 1 onion directly over a flame to brown it and then stud it with cloves. It will flavor and color the stock (this was Madame Charigot's special trick). Fill a cooking pot with 4 quarts of water and drop in the vegetables together with the giblets. Cover and bring rapidly to the boil. Skim as often as

necessary. When the liquid is clear add the bouquet garni, ginger and white wine. Season with salt and, only at the end, pepper. Simmer over a very low heat for 3 hours at least. Strain the stock and keep at low temperature until it is used.

The vegetables and the cooked meat (which was scraped off the bones and skin) can be prepared as delightful salad served with a simple oil and vinegar or *rémoulade* (mustard) dressing.

LA ROUÏA
ROUILLE

For 6 people

2 red peppers; 2 garlic cloves; coarse salt; 1 cup olive oil; 1 slice stale bread; stock.

Cut open the red peppers and remove the seeds, then rinse and chop the flesh. Peel the garlic. Crush the red peppers and garlic in a mortar, adding a pinch of salt and a tablespoon of olive oil.

Remove the crust from the bread and moisten the soft part with stock. Add the moistened bread to the mix of peppers and garlic. Continue grinding, while slowly pouring the rest of the oil into the mortar, until the paste has the consistency of mayonnaise. If it separates, add a teaspoon of very hot stock. Just before serving, beat some stock into the rouille (four or five parts stock to one part rouille). In place of the bread, you can use a slice of well-cooked potato if you prefer.

Rouille is traditionally served with bouillabaisse, but it can also be served with a chicken dish, diluted with chicken stock.

SAUCE NANTUA
NANTUA SAUCE

For 6 people

1 pint béchamel sauce (see recipe on this page); 1 cup light cream; salt and ground white pepper; 1 pinch cayenne pepper; ¹/₂ cup crayfish bisque.

Heat up the béchamel sauce in a small cooking pot. Once it is steaming hot, add half the cream. When the mixture starts to boil, lower the heat and cook until it is reduced by about two-thirds its initial volume. Mix in the rest of the cream, season and heat up the sauce, stirring continuously. Remove from the heat and add a spoonful of butter or crayfish bisque prepared from finely ground shells and stock. Serve in a preheated sauceboat. The sauce can be kept warm or reheated using a double boiler. This recipe can also be prepared using bass, perch or pike.

SAUCE BÉCHAMEL LÉGERE
LIGHT WHITE SAUCE

For 6 people

1 pintl milk, heated; 1 bouquet garni with parsley stalks; 1 onion studded with a clove; white peppercorns; 6tbsp butter; ¹/₄ cup sifted flour; salt and white pepper.

Boil the milk and add the bouquet garni, the onion and the peppercorns to infuse.

Melt the butter over a low heat in a heavy-based saucepan. Add the flour all at once and stir immediately with a wooden spoon until the mixture starts to foam and turn white. Keep stirring over a low heat for about 4 to 5 minutes until it is smooth. Remove from the heat, add the hot milk, after removing any skin, and whisk vigorously to achieve a homogenous texture, taking care the sauce does not curdle. Place over a low heat and add salt and pepper. Simmer for about 10 minutes, stirring continuously. If the sauce is not to be served at once, trail a piece of chilled butter on the surface while it is still hot to prevent a skin forming.

CREME ANGLAISE ET ILES FLOTTANTES
CUSTARD AND SNOW EGGS

For 6 people

1 vanilla bean; 1¹/₂ quarts milk; 12 egg yolks (weighing about 2¹/₂ oz each); 1³/₄ cups sugar; pinch of salt; 12 egg whites; 3¹/₂ cups confectioner's sugar.

Break the vanilla bean in half and drop it into the milk. Bring the milk to the boil slowly, and simmer long enough for the vanilla to flavor it.

Prepare a double boiler using a stainless steel mixing bowl and place over medium heat. Drop in the egg yolks, add the sugar and, using a wooden spoon to blend, whisk until the contents turn white and thicken. Then leave to cool. (This is not the usual way of preparing custard but it gives a creamier texture). Slowly pour in the steaming hot milk while stirring rapidly.

In a double boiler, patiently stir the custard, always in the same direction, until it is thick enough to coat the spoon. Remove from the double boiler and continue to stir until completely cool. The French colloquial term for this process is "*vanner*" ("to be dead beat"), a rather pertinent expression since the creamy texture can only be achieved through beating. To speed up the process, immerse the mixing bowl into a container of water chilled with ice cubes as soon as the custard is removed from the heat.

Take out the vanilla pieces. Rinse them well, without soaking, and pat dry; they can be used again. Caramel, coffee, chocolate, rum can also be used to flavor the custard.

Custard is in itself a dessert. It is also the best "float" for Snow Eggs, prepared from the set-aside egg whites. To make these, add a pinch of salt to the egg whites and beat until stiff. Slowly sprinkle in the confectioner's sugar and fold in gently. Then drop large individual ladlefuls of egg whites into a pan of simmering milk. Another option is to prepare a caramel-coated round cake pan and fill it with egg whites. Using a double boiler, cook for about 20 minutes in a preheated oven on a low heat 200°F. Remove from the mold and cut the caramelized cake into slices.

CARAMEL

Away from the heat, mix together $^1\!/_4$ cup of cold water, $^2\!/_3$ cup of sugar and a few drops of lemon juice. Let it sit for 10 minutes for the sugar to dissolve before placing it over a low heat. Let the sugar brown, without stirring. Make sure it does not turn too dark in color. Roll the caramel along the sides of the hot mold or, if a saucepan was used, transfer quickly into a mold.

*D*rawing by Renoir
for Mme Charpentier.
Private collection.

Recipes

Photography Credits

Acknowledgements

*I would like to thank the Galleries, Antique Dealers, and Boutiques
who kindly lent me the objects needed for this book.
Thanks for their support to: Aux Fils du temps, Fanette, Éric Dubois,
Au Puceron Chineur, la Tuile à loup, Les Deux Orphelines, L'Herminette, la Table en fête,
la Maison ivre, Elsa Halfen, J.P.L.D antiquités, le Cochelin au Louvre des Antiquaires,
Art domestique ancien, Fuchsia linge et dentelles anciens, Suger au Louvre des Antiquaires,
Mère-Grand, Dominique Paramythiotis Gallery, Anne Vincent, L'Or du temps,
Josy Broutin Gallery, L'Ourartien, Darlay, L'Autre jour–Dorothée D'Orgeval,
la Galerie Pittoresque au Louvre des Antiquaires, Kin Liou, Un Soupçon de charme (Orléans),
Alexandre Biaggi, Garance, Haga, Au Bain Marie, Bernardaud Porcelaine, Des Fleurs, Ariodante,
Derrière la porte, Mokuba, l'Argenterie des Francs-Bourgeois, Acanthe et Jean Louis Riccardi,
Antoine Coti Gallery, Segries, Le Marquisat, Siècle, Noël, Christophe d'Aboville,
Didier Ludot Gallery, Muriel Grateau, Marie-Laurence Nusse.*

Lydia Fasoli

*Special thanks to the staff of Le Petit Riche and Fournaise restaurants.
Thanks also to Pierre Mauduit who photographed* Le Diplomate *and* le Gâteau au chocolat
especially for this book.

*We also wish to thank
France Daguet, Sylvie Delassus, Anne Distel, Mme Escoffier-Robida,
Mme Flandrin-Robida, M. Froumessole,
Caroline Godfroy Durand-Ruel, Brigitte Kueppers.
and
the Gorne Laboratory
for their collaboration in the development of the films.*

*Thanks to Cory McCloud for the layout and
to Sian Ascott, Catherine Barry, Mélusine Klein, Nick Lezard, Bill Niven, Cathy Muscat
for their collaboration on the English edition.*